A
Woman's
Place
is in
the House

To Lee,
Many thanks
for your contribution
to this book.
Best wishes,
Hilary.

A
Woman's
Place
is in
the House

Hilary
Baxter

This book is dedicated to:

Roger Stotesbury

a continuing inspiration

Contents

Foreword

Having known Hilary Baxter as my constituent for two decades, it is no surprise to me that she has produced this outstanding piece of scholarship and writing on the need for gender equality in the House of Commons. The book reflects her painstaking effort, meticulous research, and deep passion for progressive change.

As Hilary demonstrates, equality does matter and we are still a long way off it, notwithstanding major steps forward over the last two decades. Charting the motivation of women entering politics, the different way in which female members often go about the role of Parliamentary representation and the measures most likely to increase it, Hilary has laid down a challenge to all who want something better than the status quo and need a dependable tool kit to deliver it.

I warmly welcome the book, hope that you will enjoy reading it, and urge those who accept its messages to act to ensure that they are delivered in the decade ahead.

Rt Hon John Bercow MP
Speaker of the House of Commons and Member of Parliament for Buckingham

Introduction

Currently, the UK is 38th in the world for parliamentary gender equality (latest figures January 2018), down from 25th place in 1999. The UK now lies behind countries like Rwanda, Bolivia, Senegal, and South Africa on women's political representation. Most developing countries have put quotas in place for women, recognizing the age-old and ongoing barriers that they have to battle against.

The use of quotas has transformed national policy in these countries. In Senegal, a greater share of the country's GDP is now allocated to education. In Rwanda, laws have been passed that protect children from violence and allow women to own land. In Ecuador, female MPs are more likely to introduce bills relating to education, health, and the environment.

Meanwhile, the UK persists with the idea of MPs being appointed on a level playing field via meritocracy, when all evidence suggests we are in a post-apartheid environment. There are and have always been dozens of mediocre male MPs, so let us not delude ourselves that the current system gets the best. The UK is not progressing towards equality as fast as other nations, and it is going backwards relative to many.

At the current rate of improvement, the UK will have to wait another 90 years before it gets 50:50 representation in the Commons, and even longer for the Lords. In the past two years in the House of Commons, bills that protect women, such as the Domestic Violence Bill, have been vehemently opposed by some male MPs (e.g. Philip Davies), whilst others have campaigned for bills that could provide anonymity to men accused of rape.

We are only 47th out of 188 countries in equal judicial representation. Only two of our 12 Supreme Court judges are women, and the second was only appointed in 2017. This is a book aimed at encouraging any woman who is interested in politics and/or representative legislation who may or may not have thought about becoming an MP herself to seriously consider the need for more women MPs and why it is necessary for fair and meaningful legislation.

There is a dearth of guidance for aspiring female MPs. In these times of trolling, venomous abuse of female MPs, and the death of Jo Cox in 2016, many women are put off from going into public life. As ever, they are being intimidated and silenced by misogyny.

At the 2015 Women of the World conference in London's Southbank, after a debate by three women MPs, the panel asked the audience how many of them had considered going into politics, and a lot of hands went up. When the MPs then asked how many had actually gone into politics, all the hands went down. Reasons given were: fear, trolling and threats to family life, though as the interviews with current MPs in this book testify, nothing could be further from the truth. The MPs all say that their job is the best in the world and that trolling comprises a very minor part of it.

There needs to be positive, ongoing encouragement for women or the number of female MPs will stagnate or decline. Historic data from the World Bank shows that even the nations that have most successfully increased female representation (Scandinavian countries) have seen a decline or stagnation at around 40% of female MPs. 47% of Sweden's MPs were female MPs in 2005, and this figure had declined to 43% by 2015. In Denmark, the percentage of female MPs has not risen since

2000 and remains around 37%. In Norway, it has only risen 3%, from 36% to 39% over the last 15 years. There are few practical or positive books inspiring more women to go into Parliament and explaining why more women are needed. This is such a book.

Why does it matter?
It's 2019, but male MPs outnumber female MPs by 2:1 in the Commons and 3:1 in the Lords. Of the current 650 seats, men hold 442 (68%) and women hold 208 (32%). Every decision made in Parliament impacts the nation's daily life. It is for this simple reason that there should be fair representation of the public around the legislative table. At the current rate of change, this means another 90 years of a majority male Parliament making the key legislation for the entire UK population. Would men tolerate a majority of women writing laws for them?

When we look at what has happened when men made laws in the past, we can see the resulting unfair laws regarding pensions, the tampon tax, mortgages, marriage certificates, rape, sex trafficking, maternity leave, childcare, and domestic violence, to name but a few. How different would these laws have been if they had been written by a gender-balanced team?

The Equal Pay Act was written by men in 1970, and it has failed. Forty-nine years after this act, why do we still have a 15% to 20% pay gap in the UK? Why are women having to fight major organizations like the BBC, Tesco, ASDA, and Glasgow City Corporation for equal pay? If this is happening in large publicly funded and apparently accountable organizations, what pay inequalities are happening elsewhere across the UK? Why isn't equality legislation working?

The Sex Discrimination Act was written by men in 1975. This also failed and had to be replaced by the Equality Act of 2010. Why, in January 2018, were events like the President's Club charity dinner still being exposed? Why is this discrimination still happening in the UK in the 21st century? Though the legislation has improved, we are still living in a deeply unequal society, set by gender stereotyping even before birth, which dictates very different life chances for most people that are primarily dependent on their sex.

When women are missing from key roles in public life, their status diminishes in society and laws are written and enacted without a thought for one half of the population. Once on the statute book, these laws can take centuries to be changed. Look at marriage certificates. Why is it only now, in the 21st century, that we are finally agreeing that the mother's name should be on this document? And yet it still hasn't happened. This legislation dates back to Victorian times when women had little to no rights, but it still hasn't been fixed.

When debating a Bill, the Speaker of the House has to choose an archaic hierarchy of speakers, which means that the chairs of committees and the longest-serving MPs get chosen ahead of anyone else. If they choose to filibuster or "drone on", then bills can run out of time and never reach the statute book, and younger, newer, more dynamic, and often female MPs have little chance of being heard.

The Select Committees of both houses have no requirement to be gender balanced, and so 32 out of 36 Commons and 29 out of 32 Lords Select Committees are majority male. How shameful is it that one, white, male, pale and very stale MP (Christopher Chope) can filibuster a Bill designed to stop women from being up-skirted? This is a man who never has and never will experience such a degrading event.

Women of the UK cannot afford to allow a majority male Parliament to write the key laws governing their lives for another 90 years. With the UK leaving the EU, most of our social legislation is being re-written and the likelihood is that a majority of men will not be looking at the impact of their legislation on women. There is often no conspiracy amongst men to consider women; it just doesn't occur to them since it is outside their experience and just becomes the law of unforeseen circumstances.

The political landscape is in deficit without more talented women. Simply deciding where the majority of taxpayers' money is spent is key to jobs and the future direction of the country. Male MPs are historically known for spending more money on defence and large infrastructure projects, which also (unsurprisingly) favour jobs for men. Female MPs are more likely to be concerned with health, education, the community, and the environment. Investment in care creates twice as many jobs as investment in construction.

McInsey estimates that bridging the UK gender gap in work would create an extra £150bn on top of GDP forecasts by 2025. This could translate into an extra 840,000 women getting into work. At least 600,000 stay-at-home parents would prefer to work if they could afford to do so. The Women's Business Council estimated in 2012 that there were 2.3m women who wanted to be in work but weren't and a further 1.3m who wanted to work more hours.

If legislation were put in place to provide universal free childcare for all parents in the UK from the end of maternity/paternity leave, the economy would benefit by

£1.5bn in increased tax revenues and decreased benefits for every 10% of extra parents (mostly mothers) in work. Yet majority male governments have continued to ignore this obvious benefit because they view childcare as a cost and as a female "problem" rather than as a benefit to all of society. We need to open the doors to female talents and experience. If we do so, Parliament will be a better place, legislation will be better, and the country will thrive.

Chapter 1

Why female representation matters

When Harriet Harman won her by-election in Peckham in 1982, 37 years ago, there were only 23 other women MPs, comprising 3.5% of the total of 650. The number of women MPs had not been increasing since 1945, when there were 24, and in fact, they had reached the dizzy height of 29 women MPs in 1964. It had generally been accepted that the number of female MPs had flat-lined and that women had achieved about as much representation as they could expect.

Fortunately, Harriet saw it differently, and every woman in the UK today owes her a lot for the tireless and bloody-minded battles she fought on all our behalves against entrenched male opposition from within her own party as well as from the Tories. The single greatest battle she won was getting all-women shortlists accepted by the Labour Party for the 1997 election.

It's too easy to forget what life was like back then, remembering the programmes we had to stomach nightly on the BBC. *Ken Dodd's Showbiz*, *Mike Yarwood In Person*, Benny Hill, Eric Sykes, Morecambe and Wise, and Kenny Everett, all white, male, pale and stale, give us a taste...the sexist mother-in-law jokes came thick and fast together with a stereotype of stay-at-home housewives, tarted-up and waiting for the milkman's visit as their highlight of the day. Professional, career women were nowhere to be seen on mainstream TV, or anywhere else, for that matter.

Yes, there was a woman Prime Minister, Margaret Thatcher, who had succeeded against all the odds. But because she'd overcome the childcare and sexist battles herself, she expected other women to do so too. Sadly, not all other women had such supportive husbands or the necessary income. When Harriet asked about the lack of childcare provision during school holidays[1] "as most parents work to support their families", Margaret replied: "No, I do not believe that it is up to the government to provide care for schoolchildren during the school holidays". Incredibly, this was accepted reasoning in those days, and it was poor Harriet who was humiliated, not just by the opposition, but also by her own side.

But Harriet was made of tougher stuff and didn't give up, despite being told that if she spoke out on feminist issues, she would be sidelined for the rest of her career. She founded the Women's Parliamentary Labour Party Group for her fellow ten female colleagues. There was fierce anti-women, anti-feminist feeling amongst the male Labour ranks in those days. "It was all mines, motorways and money supply[2]" Harman says of the 1980s, with little to no discussion of issues that affected one half of the population. Harriet, also known as the "Mother of the House", has made more impact – not just on parliament, but on women's lives everywhere in the UK – than any other politician (male or female) of her generation.

As Shadow Employment Minister, Harriet fought for Labour's adoption of the national minimum wage, since most of the low-paid are women. She created the Low Pay Commission, opposed by union leaders who protested that it undermined their collective bargaining. Barbara Castle had faced the same union objections over equal pay decades earlier. Male Labour MPs fought hard against Harriet's all-women shortlists, which changed the male face of the Commons in the 1997 election when there was a giant leap forward for womankind: from 60 to 120 female MPs, or from 9.2% to 18.2%. We can all remember the shot of Tony Blair and his "Blair Babes" which revolutionized female representation in Parliament.

Fast-forward to debates in the Commons this year – which have included personal experiences of abortion expressed by individual female MPs, the tampon tax, period poverty, FGM, sexual harassment, state-provided childcare for 30 hours per week, and the reading out of the names of the 100+ women who are killed by their partners each year – and you realize just how far we have moved forward with women's issues. For too long, the issues of 51% of the population have been ridiculed and ignored by successive generations of the 90%+ male MPs in Parliament and the House of Lords, who simply had no understanding of women's lives and how these issues really matter to women.

Some men might say that these debates on women's issues are a backward step and that they would be happier going back to discussing guns, roads, and interest rates. But Parliament needs to be inclusive and to have debates on the concerns of all constituents. Only by getting a tipping point of sufficient numbers of women MPs has the dialogue changed, with 32% of MPs now being female (as of the June 2017 election) giving enough courage by numbers to allow female MPs to speak out and be helped by supportive voices. We haven't moved far enough, but the very fact that these issues are being openly discussed with respect and sympathy shows that we have come a long way.

Gender quotas around the globe
Drude Dahlerup, a Danish-Swedish Professor at Stockholm University, has done a lot of research on the impact of gender

quotas around the world. In her book: *Has Democracy Failed Women?*[3] she writes: "No-one had predicted the rapid spread of gender quotas in electoral systems to over half the countries in the world. Today [in 2018], more than eighty countries as diverse as Bolivia, South Korea, India, France and Uganda, have by law adopted gender quotas for their elected assemblies". It is intriguing that this has happened against a backdrop of male-majority parliaments, who must have known that these quotas would have a negative impact on them.

The reasons are threefold: women's interest groups on a national and international scale have exerted pressure, most parliaments now wish to look modern and representative, and legislation is given more credence when it is seen to have been written and passed by a representative parliament.

There are three different types of gender quota:
a) party candidate quotas, adopted by individual parties and usually voluntary (mostly in Europe)
b) legislated candidate quotas, where the law requires that parties have a minimum percentage of women amongst the candidates on their lists (mostly Africa and Latin America)
c) reserved seats mandated in constitution or law (mostly Middle East and India)

India
In India, in 1993 a constitutional amendment made it mandatory for Indian states to decentralize a significant amount of policy influence to a three-tier system of local governance. This amendment required that one third of leader positions be reserved for women. A review of the impact of this legislation gives three conclusions: (1) quotas can and do increase female leadership in politics, (2) female leadership

influences policy outcomes, and (3) gender quotas do not seem to create a sustained backlash amongst citizens.

However, groups who are adversely affected – male incumbents and party leaders – respond strategically to reduce the impact of gender quotas. The British Labour Party is a good example: having increased its number of female MPs in 1997, the Party's male hierarchy has acted strategically ever since to ensure they have had no female leader, with the exception of Harriet Harman as Acting Leader for a short time.

Sweden
In Sweden, there is no legal requirement for quotas, but the Greens, the Left Socialists, and the Social Democratic Party apply the zipper system, where they nominate 50% men and 50% women on their lists for election, alternating between men and women throughout the list.

Morocco
In Morocco, 60 of the 395 seats are reserved for women and 30 seats for young people of both sexes under 40, and they are elected by all voters on the basis of special national lists. The voters have two votes, one for the national list and one for the district seat.

UK
Currently, the UK is 39th in the world for parliamentary gender equality (Inter-Parliamentary Union, February 2019), down from 25th place in 1999. The UK now lies behind countries like Rwanda, Bolivia, Senegal, and South Africa on women's political representation, and none of these countries have been noted for their gender equality in the past, which doesn't say good things about the UK. Most developing countries have

put in place quotas for women, recognizing the age-old and ongoing barriers that women have to battle against.

The use of quotas has transformed national policy in these countries. In Senegal, a greater share of the country's GDP is now allocated to education. In Rwanda, laws have been passed that protect children from violence and allow women to own land. In Ecuador, female MPs are more likely to introduce bills relating to education, health, and the environment.

All-women shortlists in the UK

There was a huge backlash against the concept of all-women shortlists in the UK, with many stating how it was demeaning to women, discriminatory against men, and meant that low-quality women could be parachuted into posts in preference to higher-achieving men. How unfair; like this hadn't been happening throughout the course of history in favour of men? No-one had complained during the last 200 years how the all-male shortlists might be discriminating against women, meaning that low-quality male MPs got into post by the hundred and stayed for 25 to 30 years.

There has been forensic analysis of the 101 female MPs who took advantage of this once-in-a-lifetime opportunity and how they have fared in Parliament since. According to "The 'Blair Babes': Where Are They Now?"[4] and "Blair Babes 'Have Failed' Women in Politics"[5], they have either...

...failed other women by focusing on their own selfish needs (why should they object to all-night sittings? Surely they knew it was going to be like this when they stood for Parliament?), rather than furthering the cause of women in general. They were subjected to sexist attacks and ridiculed in the press and their qualifications were questioned. They were severely chastised for following the party whip when later in 1997, they voted for budget cuts on lone mothers' benefits. In "Too Spineless to Rebel? Labour's new Women MP's",[6] it was noted that they were half as likely to defy the party whip on any issue. Sixty-five of the intake were new MPs who were criticized for being "too careerist" and focused on their own progression rather than caring about the future of ordinary women on the street. Have male MPs have ever been criticized like this en masse or their qualifications questioned?

....or they've done pretty well, considering what they were up against at the time: no maternity leave, all-night sittings, bullying, harassment, media misogyny, 18 bars but no nurseries or childcare on the Westminster site, and, in 2016, the cold-blooded killing of Jo Cox.

Of the 101 "Blair Babes", this is what happened[7]:
17 are still sitting MPs;
9 retired or lost their seat in 2001;
22 retired or lost their seat in 2005;
37 retired or lost their seat in 2010;
8 retired or lost their seat in 2015;
2 retired or lost their seat in 2017;
6 have died.

Seven arguments for and against quotas
Taken from Fig 3.2 Professor Drude Dahlerup's excellent book *Has Democracy Failed Women?*

Opponents Predictions	Proponents Predictions
Quotas are unnecessary, as women's representation will increase gradually in a natural way	Quotas are necessary, to achieve a rapid increase in women's political representation
It won't be possible to find a sufficient number of qualified women. And women won't want to be selected because of their sex.	There will be a sufficient number of qualified women candidates, if political parties look harder for women
Quotas are a violation of the free choice of the voters, they are demeaning to women and will undermine the principle of merit	Quotas will enlarge the pool of potential candidates, making better use of diverse qualifications in society
Women elected via quotas will only be seen as "quota women" and their political effectiveness will consequently be limited	A critical mass of women will bring a different style and approach to politics
Quota women will be regarded as "token" or "proxy" women, too dependent on their party leaders or husbands	A critical mass of women will introduce new policy concerns into the political agenda
After gender quotas, other groups will start demanding quotas, such as ethnic minorities, left-handed people and even redheads!	Gender is one of the most important axes of power in society. Gender quotas are therefore not only necessary but essential.
Quotas only treat the symptoms of women's under-representation and so will only be a symbolic gesture	Quotas will contribute to the process of democratization by opening up the "secret garden of politics".

The critical mass theory

The common view is that it takes a certain percentage of women in politics (or on boards or committees) to make a difference. One lone or token woman will behave like the male majority, for fear of ridicule and lack of support for her views. It is generally accepted that there needs to be 30% to 35% of women in a room, meeting, or committee to make a difference by giving women enough courage to speak out and supporting each other. Interestingly, this doesn't seem to be the case for men from ethnic minorities, one of whom seems perfectly capable of speaking out on behalf of his interest group.

Do men from ethnic minorities inherently have more courage than women? Probably very likely, since they won't have been subjected to the sexual bullying and intimidation that all women experience from birth onwards.

Do more women MPs = more female- friendly legislation?

In Europe, it has been hard to prove a causal link between an increased number of female MPs and female-friendly legislation. Even in Scandinavia, where typically at least 40% of MPs are women, the causal link to the extended welfare systems such as free childcare is hard to prove.

The policy effect of increased numbers of women MPs also depends on the context, the commitment of the politicians, and the positions of women and feminists in the hierarchies of power. Also on, how relatively easy it is to write new legislation and get it passed into law. As we know in the UK, this is not an easy process. For example, large amounts of (mostly female) MPs' time has been devoted over the last few years to improving pensions for women. As the existing pension laws were based on the full- time (male) employment model for many years and women taking time out to have babies lost out on their pension income. Nearly a quarter of single female pensioners live in poverty, and of those who live in couples, the woman on average is only getting 32p for every £1 her husband or /partner gets[8].

Despite best efforts, especially on behalf of the Women Against State Pension Inequality (WASPI[9]) campaign, little progress has been made. One could either conclude that the female MPs just haven't been up to the job, or that there has been effective obstruction by other MPs driven to save the existing state pension pot which is short of funds, or that changes to complex pensions law are beyond the wit of most people and too difficult to bring into law, or a combination of all of these factors. No-one has been trying to obstruct the WASPI campaign, but as we have seen with all sorts of legislation, once things are on the statute book, they become hard to change.

Look at the lack of provision for the mother's name on a marriage certificate. This was first written into law during Victorian times when women had few rights or regard, but it has taken (to date) 120 years to try and rectify this wrong and it still has not been done, despite David Cameron pledging to rectify this historical anomaly back in 2014. Mother's names are still not being recorded on marriage certificates because Parliament still finds more pressing issues to discuss. I ask any reader who is a mother and might find herself in this situation to write her name all over the marriage certificate of her son or daughter to make a point. Of course, because most women are compliant and don't wish to ruin their daughter or son's wedding day, they won't, and so the injustice carries on.

As Professor Drude Dahlerup explained in her book: "Women's Parliamentary representation today is almost the same in

17

democratic regimes, as in semi-democratic or authoritarian regimes. This is the result of the adoption of electoral gender quotas by all types of political regimes, especially post-conflict countries, which have offered opportunities for the dislocation of some of the old male political elites, especially in Africa. Today we see the importance of the mobilization of women for the emergence of new democratic regimes".

The raising of female representation to a critical mass percentage of 30% and above has only been achieved in some democracies within the last 20 years. Interestingly, major social change and especially female-friendly legislation with a focus on children's and mother's health and education has been more noticeably enacted in post-conflict African nations, such as Rwanda, than in the older democracies of Europe. Although admittedly this is because many African nations (including Rwanda) were further behind on these policy areas.

But is it really possible to change a patriarchal regime through more female MPs and via legislation? In tandem to this, there needs to be a strong judiciary with good female representation to interpret and uphold a law from a female perspective (rape, maternity laws, and sexual harassment and bullying spring to mind) and also a change in societal attitudes and the media, in terms of how they represent legal change and the outcome of test cases.

Also, now that the world is becoming increasingly globalized, it is important that global agencies such as the UN, World Bank, European Commission, G20, and G8 get better female representation. For too long, photos of the G8 or G20 leaders have shown nearly all men, with the exception of Angela Merkel.

Anneliese Dodds, MP for Oxford East, was born in Aberdeen in 1978 and studied Politics, Philosophy, and Economics at St Hilda's College, Oxford. She graduated with a first class degree and then got a Master's Degree from the University of Edinburgh, followed by a PhD in Government at the London School of Economics. She was a member of the European Parliament for the South East Region in 2014 and sat on the European Parliament's Committee on Economic and Monetary Affairs. She was elected Labour MP for Oxford East in the June 2017 snap election and a month later she was made Shadow Treasury Minister.

"It is vital that we get to a 50:50 gender split because we need a Parliament that is more representative of society which includes gender, racial diversity, and social class, and it's not going to happen by accident. You need rules and mechanisms and procedures. One area ripe for change is that very rarely do we consider the impact of tax and spending decisions on real women. So changes made since the recession, especially changes to social security, have had a significant impact, with over 80% of the cuts applying to women. It's had a particular impact on lone parents, and the major proportion of them are women. The Department of Work and Pensions has had a subservient relationship to the Treasury, whereas if we had a better relationship, then we'd realise it's not just about pay for women, but about social security too".

Jo Swinson is a Scottish Liberal Democrat politician and MP for East Dumbartonshire. She was first elected in the 2005 general election, serving until her defeat by the SNP ten years later. She regained her seat in the 2017 snap general election with a majority of 5,339 votes. She was the Parliamentary Under Secretary of State for Employment Relations, Consumer, and Postal Affairs. She was formerly a junior Equalities Minister, and in June 2017, she was elected unopposed as the Deputy leader of the Liberal Democrats. In July 2019 she became the first ever female Leader of the Liberal Democrats.

Jo is down-to-earth, and has a soft non-confrontational voice, having you eating out of her hand in minutes. She was educated in a mixed state comprehensive school in Milngavie. She took the time to speak to me just days before she gave birth to her second child. With an 800-mile round trip by train to her constituency in Paisley every week, with two very young children, her dedication to public service is inspiring.

"It's important to get to 50%, or pivoting between 45% to 55% between men and women. It matters because different people bring their own lived experiences to Parliament. Then Parliament will be a better body not only because it has more diverse groups that can challenge dogmatically held positions, but also to more fully represent the different experiences that people in the country are actually having".

"This matters in terms of gender, but it also matters in terms of race, socio-economic class, income, and different occupations that people might have had before coming into Parliament, and different ages, and across a whole range of issues, we want to have a more representative Parliament, which will be stronger".

"With more women MPs in place, particularly since 1997, a wider range of issues has been given prominence, from childcare to domestic violence to sexual harassment, issues around women's health and reproductive rights. Men can raise these issues, but certainly they were seen as more fringe before there were significant numbers of women in

Parliament. Issues that generally affect women are more likely to be marginalized or termed 'soft issues'".

"Women bring a different perspective to all issues, so we're not looking at everything through the male lens. Although sympathetic to the cause of period poverty, FGM, abortion, and safety on the tube going home, most men simply can't relate to these issues from a personal perspective, so it's down to women to speak up, not be ashamed of them, and recognize they are speaking on behalf of half the population, who will benefit from changes in these basic issues. To be fair, men are sympathetic when these topics are brought up; many just didn't know of their existence until recently".

Caroline Spelman is a Conservative Party politician and MP for Meriden in the West Midlands. Caroline was born and grew up in Hertfordshire and got a first class BA in European studies from Queen Mary College, University of London. She was sugar beet commodity secretary for the National Farmers Union from 1981 to 1984. She was then Deputy Director of the International Confederation of European Beet Growers in Paris from 1984 to 1989.

"We do desperately need more women in politics. All the hard evidence is that better decision-making happens when men and women are both involved. The illustration I always give of this, because this makes people get it, is: if you look at public transport and you ask men what are the most important things to consider, they will say price and reliability, whilst women put something completely different as top, which men don't even consider or think of putting on the list, and that's safety".

"So you see, if you put the three together: safety, value for money, and reliability, you get a better answer. And people go 'ah yes, I hadn't really thought of that.' And you could go to every subject area and find those little nuances. And enlightened companies know that their boards are better if they are more diverse. I sit on the board of Commonwealth Games England, and the games are going to Birmingham in 2022, so I'm going to try and help them succeed in their local area. We've got a very diverse board: we are 50:50 men and women, which is great, because there are a lot of empowered women in the sports sector. We've also got two paraplegics, and we've got two black and minority ethnic board members. Our decision-making is so much better for this, it is really heartening".

Jeremy Paxman used her case as an illustration in his book *The English* as an example of how it is still difficult for women to get into politics. Caroline was turned down by 27 constituencies before finally getting selected to stand for Bassetlaw constituency in Nottinghamshire in the 1992 general election, although she lost. She was then selected to stand for Meriden in the West Midlands, where she won the seat in 1987, and has been an MP for over 20 years as well as a former Cabinet Minister (for the Environment). Her constituency covers rural Warwickshire with horse-owning wealthy landowners and one of the poorest estates in Europe, so she has a challenging tightrope to walk to keep all of these people happy.

Laws (or lack of them) that have failed women
Legislation covering equal pay, sexual discrimination, rape, sexual harassment, pensions, FGM, health research, education policy, media coverage, universal credit, marriage, caring in the home, transport, violence against women, childcare provision...these laws have all failed women and children.

State-funded childcare for all in Scandinavia
Enlightened Scandinavian countries with higher numbers of
female MPs have enacted legislation that provides state-
funded free (or very low cost) childcare for all parents from the
birth of their child onwards. These countries have recognized
the economic benefits of this for everyone. In 1975, the
Swedish government made public daycare available and
affordable to all. In most municipalities, parents who stay at
home receive no benefits, so they are rewarded and enabled
to go out to work.

The knock-on effect of this non-discriminatory universal free
childcare can be seen throughout Swedish society, with
women better paid and represented at all levels. It underpins
everything they do. Yes, they pay more taxes, but that is
because it is recognized that having children and bringing up
future generations in well-run childcare operated by trained
specialists benefits everyone.

The UK has some of the world's most costly childcare
By contrast, the UK has some of the most expensive childcare
in the world. And because there isn't enough provision, most
places are taken by full-time babies and children, so that it is
often impossible for women to work part-time and have
childcare provided. McKinsey estimated that if all women
could play an identical part in the economy to men, it would
add $12 trillion or 11% to global GDP by 2025[10].

Even for mothers prepared and able to go back and work full-
time, the state currently only funds up to 30 hours a week of
childcare **when the child reaches its third birthday.** So a new
mother who has finished maternity leave at, say, three or six
months and wants to go back to work full-time is faced with

the following choice (figures based on average salary for women in the UK in 2018 of £22,381):

Full-time income = £22,381
Minus tax & NIC = £3,200
Take-home pay = £18,800
Full-time childcare costs (£5/hour) or £250pw or £1k pm or £12k pa

So, childcare costs **TWO-THIRDS** of the average UK woman's salary (in fact, probably more, since no pension contributions are taken into account in the above example, probably because she can't afford it).

Childcare in London is even worse with typical costs being £1,800 per month full-time and £400 per month for wrap around care (breakfast club and after school club), meaning parents are having to pay £2,200 per month for two children, one at nursery and one at school. (actual 2019 costs)

In the author's own anecdotal experience of quizzing friends and colleagues, it's nearly always the mothers who pay for the childcare, although this is not a statistically significant sample. All the headlines say that it is the cost of childcare that puts thousands of mothers off returning to work, so the assumption is there. Perhaps some mothers are able to take the childcare cost from the joint marital account if they have one, but this is an area crying out for some research. No-one seems to know who pays for childcare in the UK, and no-one is even asking. The assumption is that it is mothers. Is this fair, when the average UK man's salary, at £32,961 is £10k pa more? Most mothers rightly perceive this as a massive motherhood penalty simply "for the right to go out and work".

Is it any surprise that so many women drop out of their careers at this point? The extra outrage is that childcare costs are not tax-deductible. Can you imagine this would be the case if men paid for childcare? The final insult is that if you work extra-long hours and need a nanny, then you have to pay employer's tax and NIC to employ her/him, so there is a double tax on a mother going out to work.

Yet if mothers give up their jobs at this point, most never get back on the career ladder and are doomed to badly paid, part-time, low-status work for the rest of their careers with the double penalty of an impoverished pension. These women's pensions will be much less because most workers depend on a private pension in order to live comfortably in old age, since the state pension is inadequate. And of course, a mother who drops out at this stage will get a much-reduced private pension too. The lifetime motherhood penalty is estimated at £407,000[11] in lost earnings. The average mother takes a pay cut of £11,000 pa when returning to work after having a baby, and if she has the baby at aged 30, then she'll have 37 more years of work after this.

By the time a mother returns to work full-time, her male partner is typically earning 21% more than her, instead of the average pay gap of 7% among childless couples, according to the Guardian report.[12] So, when she retires, her typical pension pot is just £107,000, compared with the £201,000 which is the average man's pension pot. Therefore, the cost of motherhood in reduced salary and pension is £500,000 over a lifetime.

Add in the cost of childcare, at around £11,000 pa for five years for two children, and you are looking at the eye-watering figure of a £620,000 cost of motherhood for two children. That's not including any other costs for a child, such as schooling, clothes, etc., which are estimated at an average lifetime cost of £230,000. Most fathers will pay their fair share of these other costs, but it doesn't get away from the average cost to most women of circa £500,000 to £600,000 for a lifetime of lost earnings, pensions, and childcare fees.

These costs really should be flagged up to all schoolchildren. Only then might women start choosing whether to have children from a position of knowledge, and only then might society react by improving their lot.

Would this be the case if only men bore children? No; we suspect that men would get money showered upon them for being the bearers of the next generation and doing something from which they could entirely exclude women, as they have done in most other roles throughout history.

Also, working part-time in a full-on job surrounded by full-time colleagues can be demoralizing, with the daily comments "oh, you're in today?" "I can't remember which days you are in/out?", and "you're going on holiday again when you just work part-time?" Women often have to take on their employers for the right to work part-time and then discover there are no places at the local nursery, which is oversubscribed with full-time children.

This happens because the world of work is designed around the full-time working men's model, with inconvenient "life stuff" like children, meals, ironing, and house management being taken care of by women for generations. The continuing high drop-out of women from full-time senior roles shows that not enough has changed in either society, men's attitudes, or the workplace to support them. In fact, it's getting tougher, because in today's global workplace, workers can be expected to jump on a plane at a moment's notice for a meeting elsewhere, with no thought given to competing home demands. Time for change!

Health research

For centuries, most medical research has been undertaken on men and even on male animals! The male is the default, whilst women are regarded as a deviant from the norm. The historical reason for this is that most doctors were men and were more comfortable with doing research on men because women were "less reliable due to their monthly hormonal changes". For example, the symptoms for a heart attack in medical textbooks are based on male symptoms. It is only recently that medics have begun to recognize that female symptoms can be very different.

The classic (male) symptoms of clutching at one's heart and collapsing are nothing like the female symptoms of feeling extreme nausea travelling from one's pelvis up to one's chin. This means that women who suffer heart attacks are 50% less likely to be diagnosed (because heart attacks are seen as a male issue), and even after diagnosis, they are 50% less likely to receive the correct treatment, to the extent that women are twice as likely to die in hospital from a heart attack as **men**[13]. Another example: Viagra was originally tested as a drug to control blood pressure. It wasn't very good at this , but during drug trials it was noticed the drug enabled men to have better erections and to keep them for longer. Another side effect noticed was that it stops a lot of period pain associated with menstrual cramps, but the majority male committees of researchers and doctors didn't think this was a relevant enough finding to report on it or to make it available **to women.** No further research grants were granted to explore this area.

These are just two examples of the male-dominated health profession, which traditionally gives less recognition to women's symptoms and pain. Even for pain during childbirth (which must be about the most agonizing pain known to womankind), women have been told to put up with it for as long as possible before succumbing to "artificial help". Many women's complaints to doctors about gynaecological pain or the menopause are dismissed as inconsequential. Little research has been done into the menopause, certainly in comparison to erectile dysfunction, because men never have to go through the former, whilst the latter is of deep consequence to them.

Education

The education sector has been proactive in tackling racism in the past 20 years or so. Racist comments and racist bullying in schools, colleges, and universities are treated severely and there are governors, guidance, and boards to deal with offenders. This is all to be applauded but by stark contrast, the amount of sexual harassment and attacks by males on females (by staff as well as student-on-student) is at epidemic proportions. There have been over 5,000 reported sexual offences against girls in schools in three years.[15]

The government came out with new guidelines in May 2018, after protests by two mothers who said that their daughters had been raped in school and that they wanted the recommendations by the Women and Equalities Select Committee to be implemented in full. But the government's guidelines were just that, and it's been left down to the will of each school to try and do something about this enormous problem.

From September 2020, Relationships and Sex Education (RSE) will be put on a statutory footing, which was implemented by Justine Greening, former Education Secretary. The proposals involve teaching relationship education to all primary schools and relationship and sex education to all secondary schools, although there is still a parental right of withdrawal and flexibility for schools, including faith schools, to teach within the tenets of their faith. This puts religious rights above the human rights of girls to be properly educated.

Violence against women

Two women are still killed every week by their partner or ex-partner. This statistic hasn't changed in decades. There seems little political will to do much about this. Police forces still refer to violence against women as "a domestic" rather than the grievous bodily harm that it often is. "Honour killings" are also mislabelled, since they are murder, pure and simple. Words are important. Would this be allowed if two people of colour were being killed each week simply because of their colour? The excuses and the sentences are pathetic. When technology has moved on so fast in every other sphere of life, why isn't more being done to improve life chances for women at risk? CCTV could be installed in every home where a woman and children are living at risk. This technology is cheap these days, and can be done using a mobile phone or tiny GoPro camera.

Media

The BBC, Sky, theatre, films, newspapers, the advertising industry, Youtube, Facebook, online games, social media, and online pornography all play their part in sexual stereotyping. This is the gendered society we live in;, it shapes our very perception and self-identification. If all girls see around them in the media is scantily clad young women gyrating to pop music or other forms of entertainment, with very little promotion of women doing serious jobs, valued for their brains and abilities beyond the bedroom, then is it hardly surprising that we have some very "over-gendered" young men and women today? More so than in generations brought up prior to 2000.

Today's young people learn their sex from hardcore porn, 90% of which involves some sort of violence or degradation of the woman. The coverage of women in sport is 3.2%, which is even lower than it was the 1980s[16], and only 11% of Hollywood film directors are female[17].

But not all the statistics are depressing. In Autumn 2017[18] Stage Directors UK commissioned research on the gender split of theatre directors. Some of the country's biggest theatres, including the Young Vic, the Almeida, and the Nottingham Playhouse have a more than 70:30 male/female split, but there are many, including the Royal Court and Oxford Playhouse, which have 50:50. The number of female theatre directors has increased massively in recent years, which goes to show that when organisations rely more on an older female audience who have deeper pockets and don't mind speaking out, then change can happen

In 2015, the House of Lords Select Committee on Communications produced a report on Women in the News and Current Affairs Broadcasting[19]. There were lots of excuses from the broadcasters, including the BBC, Sky, and ITN, as to why they weren't doing better, despite ongoing sexual discrimination across the board in terms of poor pay and representation for women. The BBC has had soft aspirational targets for better gender equality since the 1990s, with laughable "corporate strategic plans" talking about improving gender representation, but decades have come and gone with no obvious improvement and thousands of women's careers compromised.

The ratios of experts by topic was 4:1 in business, 5:1 in home news, 6:1 in sport, and 7:1 in all other subjects. The BBC complained that there simply weren't enough female experts, when what they meant was they hadn't looked for them. They have since been shamed into actively seeking more female experts, and in 2019 it is refreshing to listen to more female experts on a wide range of issues.

Equal pay

Justine Greening was responsible for introducing gender pay gap reporting in April 2017. This forced all companies employing over 250 people to report on their gender pay gap. There were "shock horror" headlines when the first report came out, detailing the gender pay gap across all industries with the unsurprising result that most companies had a gender pay gap in favour of men, and some of the gaps were shockingly large. The largest in retail was Phase Eight, which had a gender pay gap of 65%. It routinely directed all women onto the sales floors of its shops with consequent low pay, whilst men were directed into management positions in Head Office on higher salaries.

The third report in **April 2019**[20] showed that fewer than half of UK firms had narrowed the gap. Across 45% of firms, the discrepancy in pay increased in favour of men, while at a further 7%, there was no change. Overall, 78% of companies had a pay gap in favour of men, 14% favoured women, and the rest reported no difference. Overall, the median pay gap in favour of men lowered slightly from 9.7% in 2018 to 9.6% in 2019. There is much advice on the government website about what more companies could do to tackle this, including unconscious bias training, offering more flexible working, encouraging shared parental leave, and mentoring of more women to get them into senior management positions. Large companies with the biggest gender pay gaps included Vetcare (48.3%) and easyJet (47.9%).

The two worst industries were construction (average pay gap of nearly 25%) and finance (23%), though ironically, the biggest potential for women to secure a good salary is in these industries, if more women qualified in STEM subjects and engineering in the first place. All schoolgirls should be taught that the best salaries and jobs lie in the male-dominated industries. Administration, arts, health, accommodation, and food have the lowest pay gaps, all below 5%, but it is also worth noting that these are the worst-paying industries, which are comprised mostly of women.

This data shows that all the excuses "to get more women in the pipeline", "wait for the talented men to retire", "succession planning", and "better management training", is not providing the promised results. Why not? Because many companies are tokenistic regarding equality and are not fundamentally helping talented mothers or stopping them from leaving "when the going gets tough after childbirth".

The excuse that "women are just going to leave when they have children" is only borne out when companies and governments don't support them, and in fact, anecdotal evidence shows that a mother helped back into work and supported will be so grateful for a work/life balance that she is much more likely to remain loyal to a company for years afterwards than men, who find it easier to jump from job to job since they don't have to worry so much about childcare or a work/life balance.

Equal pay battles have been going on since the introduction of the Equal Pay Act in 1970. The women in ASDA, Tesco, and Glasgow City Council can testify to struggles that have been going on for decades, many of which still aren't resolved. The women in Glasgow City Council finally won their 13-year battle in January 2019.[21] The Tesco equal pay case could cost the supermarket up to £4bn.[22] Tesco warehouse staff (usually men) earn from between £8 and £11.50 per hour, whilst store staff (usually women) earn just £8. The disparity could mean a full-time worker earning over £5,000 a year more. It is incredible that Tesco senior management would think that a man working in the warehouse should be more highly valued than a woman dealing with customers. Many women have died just waiting for this to be sorted. They won't get any back-pay, neither will their children.

Equal representation

Women have been massively under-represented on boards for years because non-executive posts were not advertised;, it was a matter of white men choosing their pals. In 2010, Dame Helena Morrissey set up the 30PerCentClub, which had a target of making 30% of board directors female by 2020. Howard Davies then undertook a review of Women on Boards in 2011, when female representation was 22%. He set up the Women on Boards initiative in 2012, which originally had a target of Boards being 25% female by 2015.

See the review of "Where We Are At" by Cranfield University in 2016[23] . This report welcomed the fact that female representation on boards had increased, but it was mostly in the non-executive board director roles, whilst improvement in the executive positions was very slow. It is the latter that have the power. There are still only seven female CEOs of FTSE 100 companies, which has flat-lined since 2017.

Of course, the target should be 50%, but by 2019, things have improved: 28% of directors of FTSE 100 companies are now female. There is plenty of evidence which shows that companies which have more women and diversity on their boards do better financially, so why the lag to change? There is a "sticky effect" which will take generations while the UK still perceives board directors as white and male. People appoint replacements or colleagues in their own image and women often have a different style of leadership and management, which is taking a new generation and societal change to respect.

Women in local government (councils, district councils, unitary authorities, town councils, and parish councils) are better represented than at the national level. Female representation stands at about 33% in local councils and 40% in the London Assembly, and the first female metro mayor has yet to be appointed. See the Fawcett Society's "Sex and Power Report: Who Runs Britain"[24].

Women in global agencies
As the world becomes more globalized, it is argued that national parliaments have increasingly less power whilst global agencies have more. Sadly, these so-called egalitarian agencies are anything but. The UN has never had a female Permanent Secretary. They keep espousing equality whilst steadfastly overlooking all the talented women in the world and appointing men. Many of these are men of colour, just to show how egalitarian the UN is, but like the USA, which has had a non-white but no female President, race trumps sex. Surely they cannot keep arguing there isn't a talented enough woman out there amongst the 3.5bn women we have on this planet? What they mean is that they have no collective will to appoint a woman.

This chapter lays out the case for why we need better female representation throughout society, but most importantly in the areas where legislation and key decisions are made which affect the lives of everyone in the country.

References:

1. *The Guardian* (2015) [online]. Available at:
https://www.theguardian.com/politics/2015/aug/09/harriet-harman-i-think-ive-done-my-bit
[accessed 15th Nov 2018].

2. BBC Radio 4, *Woman's Hour* [online]. Available at:
https://www.bbc.co.uk/programmes/p06kytc9
[accessed 12th Sept 2018].

3. Dahlerup, D. (2018). *Has Democracy Failed Women?*
London. Polity Books.

4. BBC news [online]. Available at:
http://news.bbc.co.uk/1/hi/uk_politics/4698222.stm
[accessed 2nd Mar 2019].

5. *The Telegraph* (2000) [online]. Available at:
https://www.telegraph.co.uk/news/uknews/1349808/Blair-babes-have-failed-women-in-politics.html
[accessed 20th Mar 2019].

6. Cowley, P. and Childs, S. (2003). Cambridge University Press [online]. Available at:
http://web.pdx.edu/~mev/pdf/Cowley_Childs.pdf
[accessed 2nd Feb 2019].

7. Wikipedia (2019) [online]. Available at:
https://en.wikipedia.org/wiki/Blair_Babe
[accessed 18th Feb 2019].

8. *Daily Mail* (2018) [online]. Available at:
https://www.dailymail.co.uk/news/article-180996/Quarter-women-pensioners-poverty.html
[accessed 18th Jan 2019].

9. Women Against State Pension Inequality website (2018)
[online]. Available at: https://www.waspi.co.uk/
[accessed 20th Dec 2018].

10. McKinsey & Company (2015) [online].
Available at: https://www.mckinsey.com/featured-insights/employment-and-growth/how-advancing-womens-equality-can-add-12-trillion-to-global-growth
[accessed 23rd Sep 2018].

11. Small Business website (2017) [online]. Available at:
https://smallbusiness.co.uk/mothers-take-pay-cut-2538646/
[accessed 30th Sep 2018].

12. *The Guardian* (2015) [online].
Available at:
https://www.theguardian.com/money/2015/oct/05/childcare-expensive-mothers-want-work-trapped-home
[accessed 1st May 2019].

13. *The Express* (2018) [online].
Available at: https://www.express.co.uk/life-style/health/1049562/woman-heart-attack-fatal-twice-more-than-men-quality-treatment
[accessed 14th May 2019].

14. *Time Magazine* (2013) [online]. Available at: http://healthland.time.com/2013/12/10/study-viagra-may-relieve-womens-cramps/
[accessed 3rd May 2019].

15. BBC News (2018) [online]. Available at: https://www.bbc.co.uk/news/education-45498984
[accessed 10th April 2019].

16. Quartz (2015) [online]. Available at: https://qz.com/428680/there-is-less-womens-sports-coverage-on-tv-today-than-there-was-in-1989/
[accessed 17th Apr 2019].

17. Women and Hollywood website (2019) [online]. Available at: www.womenandhollywood.com
[accessed 20th Mar 2019].

18. Stage Directors UK website (2019) [online]. Available at: https://stagedirectorsuk.com/gender-split-of-directors-in-npos
[accessed 17th Apr 2019].

19. Parliament UK Publications (2015) [online]. Available at: https://publications.parliament.uk/pa/ld201415/ldselect/ldcomuni/91/91.pdf
[accessed 7th Dec 2018].

20. BBC News (2019) [online]. Available at: https://www.bbc.co.uk/news/business-47822291
[accessed 28th Feb 2019].

21. *The Guardian* (2019) [online].

Available at:
https://www.theguardian.com/society/2019/jan/17/glasgow-council-women-workers-win-12-year-equal-pay-battle
[accessed 3rd Feb 2010].

22. *The Guardian* (2018) [online]. Available at:
https://www.theguardian.com/business/2018/jul/11/tesco-faces-4bn-equal-pay-bill-as-claimant-numbers-swell-to-1000
[accessed 17th Jan 2019].

23. Cranfield School of Management (2016) [online].
Available at:
https://www.city.ac.uk/__data/assets/pdf_file/0003/323841/CRT054761D_Cranfield-Female-FTSE-report_Inserts_v8_HR.PDF
[accessed 12th Dec 2018].

24. The Fawcett Society Sex and Power Annual Report (2018)
[online]. Available at:
https://www.fawcettsociety.org.uk/Handlers/Download.ashx?IDMF=ea2cb329-e6e0-4e0f-8a0b-5022f99bc915
[accessed 3rd Feb 2019].

Chapter 2

"Well-behaved women seldom make history"
– Laurel Ulrich, 1976.

Why do women go into politics?

In nearly every society around the globe, with the exception of one or two matriarchal societies, like some American Indian tribes, over the last two millennia, women have been encouraged and sometimes forced to stay at home and not participate in the public space, which was men's domain. We still see this in many societies today, most notably the more religious ones, since all religions are male-dominated and suppress women.

As well as the few famous female MPs known to the public, this chapter also mentions some less well-known female MPs who deserve to be remembered in the annals of history for their contribution to progress in women's equality and society in general. In fact, they should all be getting a Victoria Cross for the courage they showed in succeeding against the stacked odds of a patriarchal society. Many would have achieved a lot more had there been more female MPs around to support them at the time and had Westminster and society in general been more receptive to female reasoning.

It takes a brave woman to put her head above the parapet.

Early pioneers

Constance Markiewicz[1] (MP 1918)

Also known as Countess Markiewicz, she was the first woman to be elected to the British House of Commons on 28th December 1918. She was also the first woman in the world to hold a Cabinet position, being Minister for Labour in the Irish Republic from 1919 to 1922.

Constance was famed for her physical courage. Born Constance Gore-Booth in London, she grew up on her father's estate in Ireland, where she became passionate about politics, due to the poverty of the workers there. She married a Polish count, Count Markiewicz, and they settled in Dublin in 1903. In due course, she became an Irish Sinn Fein and Fianna Fail politician, a revolutionary nationalist, a suffragette, and a socialist.

She took part in the Easter Rising of 1916, when Irish republicans tried to end British rule and establish an Irish Republic. She was sentenced to death, but this was reduced on the grounds of her sex. She stood for election whilst in Holloway prison. As a result, even though she won, she was unable to take up her seat in the House of Commons.

Nancy Astor[2] (MP 1919–1945)
An American citizen who moved to the UK aged 26 and married Viscount Waldorf Astor, Nancy was the first woman MP to take her seat in the British Parliament. Viscount Astor was the sitting MP for Plymouth and was elected to the peerage when his father died, so Nancy stood for the Conservatives at the ensuing by-election in 1919 and won.

Nancy devoted herself to the causes of women, children, education, and temperance. Her achievements in the House of Commons were relatively minor. She never held a position of much influence or any ministerial rank, although she did manage to secure the passage of a legal bill to increase the legal drinking age to 18.

She was outspoken and a woman of quick wit who was famed for some of her jibes with Winston Churchill: "Sir, if you were my husband, I would poison your tea", Churchill: "If you were my wife, I would drink it". She became associated with the policy of Nazi appeasement before WW2, and was persuaded to retire in 1945, as she had become a liability to her party.

Margaret Wintringham (MP 1921–1924)
The first UK-born woman to be elected and take her seat in the House of Commons, she is virtually unknown today.
She took over the seat of Lough in 1921, upon the sudden death of her husband. On the left of the Liberal Party, she fought for issues affecting women and children. Her emphasis on social issues, together with her contempt for the boorishness of the Commons, made her appear as a wild radical to many. Sadly, she lost her seat in 1924, undoubtedly due to widespread national anti-Liberal feeling.

Mabel Philipson (MP 1923–1929)
The third female MP to take up her seat in the Commons, her husband had been elected, but was forced to stand down due to fraud, and she stood in his stead at the following by-election. She was a Liberal and an advocate for women and children in need of better protection under the law. She led the Nursing Homes Registration Bill through the House and also was a key supporter of the Adoption Bill.

Katharine Stewart-Murray, Duchess of Atholl (MP 1923–1938)
The first Scottish-born woman to be elected to the Commons and the first to hold a Scottish constituency, that of Kinross and West Perthshire in 1923. She was also the first Conservative woman to hold a ministerial office as Parliamentary Secretary to the Board of Education. After hearing about FGM from the Church of Scotland Mission, she

raised the issue in the Commons, but was heckled by affronted male MPs, with red Clydesider James Maxton shouting "Is this relevant?"

She was supported by the independent MP Eleanor Rathbone, but no interest was shown by male MPs, many of whom did not believe such a practice was possible. It was to be another 50 years before Germaine Greer started talking about FGM in the 1970s. Again, she was ignored and it wasn't until actual victims like Nimco Ali started speaking up in 2010, when she founded the Daughters of Eve campaign to fight against FGM, that the establishment finally started to listen.

Dorothy Jewson (MP 1923–1924)
A visionary whose Parliamentary career was short-lived (only ten months from December 1923 to October 1924), but in that time, she advocated providing for birth control, equal voting rights for women (which still weren't the same as men until 1928), and compassion for the poorest in society. She argued that the poor should be helped with five shillings a week to keep them in their own homes, since the cost of keeping them in the workhouse would be considerably more.

Susan Lawrence (MP 1923–1931)
A passionate and determined campaigner, she made it her mission to increase state support for working class families. She emphasized the need for the agency of poor families, since she knew the Victorian-era welfare system needed radical reform. Even before becoming an MP, she was years ahead of her time, proposing reform of child labour laws back in 1915, and in 1918, she co-authored a prophetic report with William Beveridge calling for national insurance to avoid the disastrous chaos of mass unemployment at the end of WW1.

Lady Vera Terrington (MP 1923–1924)

A woman well ahead of her time, she demanded greater protection for animals, including legislation to control traps and harsher sentences for cruelty, and she campaigned against the export of live animals and stag hunting.

Margaret Bondfield[3] (MP 1923–1931)

The first woman Chair of the TUC, the first woman Cabinet Minister, and the first woman Privy Councillor. She was born in humble circumstances and received a limited education. When entering work as an embroideress, she was shocked by the working conditions and became political. She joined the NUGMW union, was elected to the TUC General Council in 1918, and became Chair in 1923.

She was elected to Parliament as Labour MP for Northamptonshire the same year, and was made Minister of Labour from 1929 to 1931. Her willingness to contemplate cuts in unemployment benefits during the great recession of the early 1930s, made her a pariah. She was considered a betrayer of the Labour movement, and to this day, she has not been forgiven, getting very little mention in the annals of Labour history.

Her main legacy was founding the Women's Group on Public Welfare, and her report published in 1943, recommended nursery education, a minimum wage, child allowances, and a national health service. This later became instrumental in developing support for the social reforms introduced by the Labour government in 1945. She also helped to launch a national drive for more women police officers.

Ellen Wilkinson[4] (MP 1924–1947)

Also known as "Red Ellen" for her fiery temperament, politics, and red hair, she was the first truly English woman to become an MP. Born into a poor though ambitious Manchester family, she embraced socialism at an early age. After graduating from the University of Manchester, she worked for a women's suffrage organization and later as a trade union officer. She was inspired by the Russian Revolution, joining first the British Communist Party and then Labour.

She became Labour MP for Middlesbrough East in 1924 and supported the 1925 General Strike. She lost her seat in 1931, but re-entered Parliament in 1935. She crusaded for the unemployed, and famously led the march of 200 unemployed workers from Jarrow to London in 1936.

She was passionate about causes for the poor. Following the 1945 election, she was made Minister of Education, and was instrumental in raising the school leaving age from 14 to 16 and introducing free school milk for all. Tragically, she died in office, in 1947 as a result of years of over-work, smoking, bronchial weakness, and an overdose of barbiturates.

Jennie Lee (MP 1929–1931 and 1945–1970)

As Minister for the Arts, she played a leading role in the foundation of the Open University, establishing the principle of open access for everyone. The existing traditional universities fought her tooth and nail, claiming that university could only be for members of the elite who had excellent qualifications, and that an Open University would belittle the value of a degree. She and the Labour government refused to be bullied into reducing the OU to college status.

Lady Megan Lloyd-George (MP 1929–1966)

Daughter of David Lloyd-George, she was the first female Welsh MP, an outspoken campaigner for a Welsh Parliament, and a consistent champion of Welsh views. She also successfully legislated for equal compensation for women and men for injuries sustained during WW2.

Lady Cynthia Mosley (MP 1929–1931)

Married to Sir Oswald Mosley, she was the second daughter of Lord Curzon, the Viceroy of India, and her mother was an American heiress with a fortune of between $25m and $30m. Selected by the Labour Party for Stoke, she won by a huge majority of 7,850. She used her own privilege to highlight those Conservative members opposing relief for the poor. "All my life I have got something for nothing. Why? Have I earned it? Not a bit". Sadly, she stepped aside for her husband, Oswald, in the 1931 election, where he was roundly beaten.

Marion Phillips (MP 1929–,1931)

Born in Australia and an MP for a mere two years, she devoted her life to the advancement of women. She pressed for public provision of baby clinics, school meals, improved council housing, employment schemes, and the prohibition of sweated labour. Elected to Parliament in 1929, she lost her seat in 1931, along with the nine other Labour women.

Edith Picton-Turberville (MP 1929–1931)

Another female MP elected in 1929, who lost her seat two years later. Her burning passion was for equality in the Church of England, campaigning for women to be ordained as priests. She was 70 years ahead of her time on this score. During her two years as an MP, she successfully introduced a law to stop pregnant women convicted of crimes being given the death penalty, through the Sentence of Death (Expectant Mothers)

Bill, and called for women to be able to serve in the police force, arguing that it would create a better social order in cities. After leaving Parliament, she continued to fight for social justice, including on the issue of Chinese refugee girls being sold into slavery in Hong Kong.

Eleanor Rathbone (MP 1929–1946)
In the 1930s, she campaigned against child marriage in India and FGM in Africa. She got family allowances onto the statute book in 1945, based on the logic that women's domestic work in the home should be valued as much as men's work outside of it.

Lady Lucy Noel-Buxton (MP 1930–1950)
Married to Noel Noel-Buxton, she stood for his seat in a by-election in 1930, when he moved to the House of Lords. She focused on colonial matters, agriculture, land rights, democracy, and education. She also participated in the Bill aimed at protecting surviving spouses or children who were left without means of support, following the deceased spouse's will or intestacy.

Dame Leah Manning (MP 1931–1950)
A passionate advocate for the teaching and welfare of children, never more so than in her hugely courageous and dramatic intervention in the Spanish Civil War, when she helped to evacuate 4,000 Basque children from Bilbao to safety in Britain. She is commemorated today with a square in Bilbao.

Thelma Cazalet-Keir (MP 1931–1945)
Her most significant act was her amendment to the 1944 Education Bill, the "Butler Education Act", which required that female teachers receive equal pay. Despite the government's

opposition to the amendment, it was passed by a single vote. Even though she was a fellow Conservative, her amendment was too radical for Churchill. He demanded it be overturned, and he made the vote a matter of confidence in the entire government. Denying women in the teaching profession equal pay was apparently so important to Churchill that he was willing to threaten the country with being left without a functioning government to achieve it, even as war still raged in Europe!

Ida Copeland (MP 1931–1935)
Elected in 1931, she was instrumental in helping the Baden-Powells to develop the Girl Guide movement.

Dame Florence Horsbrugh (MP 1931–1959She organized the evacuation of 1.5m women and children from major cities during WW2. She also brought in two Private Members' Bills, one designed to regulate adoption, the other to curb the drinking of methylated spirits in Scotland.

Mary Pickford (MP 1931–1934)
She argued for reforms to the Factories and Workshops Act, to provide a more humane and economic system of working hours for women and young people. She also focused on improving the lot of women in the world, specifically India. Her passion for social justice, women's rights, and international development were ahead of her time and could easily fit into 21st-century politics. She toured India in 1932, exploring how more women and men could be given the vote. Ninety years on, she is credited for ensuring greater rights for Indian women.

Norah Runge (MP 1931–1935)
She called for slum clearance and supported a Bill on Sunday cinema attendance. She also supported the extension of greyhound racing and protested against the inclusion of income from younger household members within the controversial means test for unemployed households.

Helen Shaw (MP 1931–1935)
She lobbied for new industries and infrastructure for her mining constituency and focused on helping ex-servicemen with the effects of economic depression and unemployment. She was also a keen airwoman and a supporter of the proposal to allow Scottish MPs to fly between London and their constituencies, a method of commuting unheard of in the 1930s.

Dame Irene Ward (MP 1931–1974)
Elected in 1931, she holds the record for the largest number of Private Members' Bills (four), including one to pay a pension of two shillings a week to elderly people living in Poor Law institutions.

Agnes Hardie (MP 1937–1945)
Known as "the housewives' MP" because of her focus on women's issues, her speeches highlighted the appalling poverty, exploitation of low-paid workers, and awful housing conditions of the time, drawing on her personal experiences of working in a shop as a trade unionist. She deserves to be remembered as a champion of the voiceless.

Dr Edith Summerskill (MP 1938–1961)
One of a few women to qualify as a doctor in the 1920s and one of the first women appointed to the Privy Council and to be made a life peer, she spent her whole life fighting for

change. In her first attempt to win a seat in Bury in 1935, she was sabotaged by Catholic priests, who denounced her for promoting birth control. Fortunately, she was undeterred and succeeded in Fulham West in 1938. She launched a campaign to ban boxing for its damage to the brain. She was devoted to the need for a publicly funded health service and called for action on poverty, nutrition, food safety, child health, and new support for miners struck down by pneumoconiosis in the 1950s.

Jennie Adamson (MP 1938–1946)
She championed the cause of women in the home. Almost every speech she made reflected the interests of working men and women, from the cost of living to, benefits for widows, orphans, and dependents of service personnel, to childcare for women who were working for the war effort. She also campaigned for the Family Allowances Bill, which had been inspired by Eleanor Rathbone.

Beatrice Wright (MP 1941–1945)
The second American-born woman to become an MP and the first to give birth to a baby whilst a serving MP. She brought her daughter to the House just two weeks after giving birth and left her in the care of a policeman whilst she voted. She made 70 speeches in her four years in Parliament, speaking on a range of issues from the war effort to women's rights and improving welfare provision.

Lady Violet Apsley (MP 1943–1945)
She highlighted the need for female architects to be involved in the design of the rural housing programme and the need for a female assistant inspector of constabulary at the Home Office to advise on the selection and training of women. As a

former officer in the Auxiliary Territorial Service, she spoke on issues facing women in the services.

Alice Bacon (MP 1945–1970)
Elected in the great Labour landslide of 1945, Alice was part of a new generation of women in Parliament, which included Bessie Braddock and Barbara Castle. Alice became a minister in 1964, playing pivotal roles in some of Labour's greatest achievements of the 1960s, including the decriminalization of homosexuality and abortion, the abolition of the death penalty, and the development of comprehensive education.

Bessie Braddock (MP 1945–1970)
A larger-than-life, working class Scouser, she fearlessly blasted her way through conventions, local and parliamentary. She always said what she thought, did what she believed to be right, and always called a spade a spade. She campaigned for improved public housing, the establishment of the NHS, and the Mental Health Act of 1959. She was an early and vigorous exponent of the MP's advice surgery; taken for granted now as part of the job, it was far from the norm in her day. Rules were never a constraint for her, and she would stop at nothing to achieve success for her constituents.

She became the first woman to be thrown out of the House for defying a ruling by the Deputy Speaker in 1952. She thought she had been promised a chance to speak and when she wasn't called, she refused to be silenced and was eventually thrown out. She was also the first woman to be thrown out of the Liverpool City Council Chamber for calling the Chair of Housing "a liar"; the police had to be called. She was an early exponent of the 'publicity stunt'.

Barbara Castle[5] (MP 1945–1979)

She was the Labour MP for Blackburn from 1945 to 1979, the longest-serving until 2007. She later became an MEP and moved to the House of Lords in 1990 as Baroness Castle of Blackburn.

She had a close working relationship with Harold Wilson, and when he became Labour leader in 1963, her prospects were transformed. She served in several cabinet roles. As Minister of Transport (1965–1968), she introduced permanent speed limits, breathalyzers, and seat belts, saving thousands of lives over the next 50 years.

As First Secretary of State (1968–1970), she successfully intervened in the strike by the Ford women sewing-machinists against pay discrimination and introduced the Equal Pay Act in 1970. During her time in government, she also served as Minister for Overseas Development and Secretary of State for Health and Social Services.

Sadly, her "in place of strife" plan, which tried to balance free collective bargaining with a commitment to full employment, fell foul of the unions, who saw it as an attack on their ability to fight for better pay and conditions. However, this does not detract from the fact that she was one of the most significant politicians of the 20th century.

Caroline Ganley (MP 1945–1951)

Aged 65 when she was first elected an MP, she spent the next six years helping to get the NHS Bill on the statute book. She called this "a glorious service to humanity".

Peggy Herbison (MP 1945–1970)
Known as "the miners' little sister", she fought passionately for the conditions of working class miners in her Scottish constituency. She was famed for her deep, clarion bell-like voice and also fought long and hard for the Labour government to increase pensions and child benefit. It was generally thought that her failure to get these measures through caused her to leave the front bench in 1967.

Jean Mann (MP 1945–1959)
A tough, working class woman and mother to five children with a long-term unemployed husband, she was a councillor in Glasgow for many years before finally becoming an MP at the age of 58. She spoke out for social welfare, arguing against austerity, and food shortages. She was passionate about improving the quality of housing and spoke strongly in favour of building low-rise housing rather than more cost-effective high-rise blocks when the Victorian tenements in Glasgow were being pulled down, though financial restrictions were against her. She was years ahead of her time on this issue and ultimately the costs of building low-rise would have been far less than the high-rise, since the latter failed massively at a social level and had to be pulled down, well ahead of the planned timeline, to be replaced by low-rise buildings.

Muriel Nichol (MP 1945–1950)
She spoke passionately for free secondary education and also urged the government to grant India its independence immediately.

Mabel Ridealgh (MP 1945–1950)
Passionate about improving appalling housing conditions for her constituents in Ilford, in 1949 she called for a minimum

wage, 50 years before it was finally introduced by a Labour government.

Harriet Slater (MP 1953–1966)
An advocate for working class women, she campaigned for better standards of education and healthcare for working class children, including the provision of playing fields and school dental care.

Dame Joan Vickers (MP 1955–1974)
A passionate backbencher, she introduced the Attachment of Income Bill, which allowed for defaults in maintenance payments (mostly by men) to be deducted from their earnings. She also introduced the Young Persons Employment Bill in 1964 and fought for the rights of prostituted women.

Margaret Thatcher[6] (MP 1959–1992)
She was the Leader of the Conservative Party from 1975 to 1990 and the longest-serving Prime Minister of the 20th century from 1979 to 1990, and the first woman to hold the office. A Soviet journalist dubbed her "The Iron Lady", a nickname that became associated with her uncompromising politics and leadership style. As Prime Minister, she implemented policies and ideals such as free market capitalism and meritocracy, which became known as "Thatcherism". She studied chemistry at Oxford, later becoming a Barrister, and was then elected MP for Finchley in 1959, despite having two young children.

She introduced a series of economic policies intended to reverse high unemployment and Britain's struggles in the wake of the Winter of Discontent (1978–1979) and an ongoing recession. Her economic policies focused on deregulation, flexible labour markets, the privatization of state-owned companies, and reducing the power of the trade unions. Her popularity in her first years in office waned amid recession and rising unemployment, until victory in the 1982 Falklands War and the recovering economy brought new support, resulting in her decisive re-election in 1983.

She survived an assassination attempt by the IRA in the Brighton Hotel bombing of 1984. Her economic policies and victory over the unions turned the British economy around and it became one of the most successful in Europe during the nineteen eighties. She was re-elected with another landslide majority for a third term in 1987, but her subsequent support for the Community Charge (Poll Tax) was widely unpopular, and her views on the European Community were not shared by others in her Cabinet. She resigned as party leader and Prime Minister in November 1990 after Michael Heseltine launched a challenge to her leadership.

Anne Kerr (MP 1964–1970)
A peace campaigner from Biafra to Vietnam, a founder of the Campaign for Nuclear Disarmament, and a champion of the fight to abolish the death penalty.

Gwyneth Dunwoody (MP 1966–1970, 1974–2008)
Nicknamed "Gunboats Gwyneth", she also received the unenviable award of "Battleaxe of the Year" from *The Oldie* magazine. She found her métier as Chair of the Transport Committee, being known for running the best Select Committee of its time and maybe possibly ever. She was more feared than any of the ministers in the department, as she focused on mismanagement, constantly questioning New Labour's mantra that the private sector "knows -best". Her high points included calling out the failings of Railtrack three years before the beleaguered Stephen Byers came to the same

conclusion. Tony Blair tried to get her sacked, since she wasn't as compliant as he wanted, but Parliament famously overturned him. This vote still stands as an important victory for Parliament, to warn all governments that they cannot manipulate Select Committees by stuffing them with "yes" men and women.

Betty Boothroyd (MP 1973–2000)

Betty was the first, and to date the only female Speaker, elected in 1992. What was just as astounding was that she was Labour and was elected when the Tories were in government. For a Tory Parliament, putting a Labour nominee in the chair was just as unprecedented as electing a woman. During her time as Speaker, she had to deal with rebellious Scottish MPs protesting in front of the mace and the resignation of a government minister, which came close to breaking the House's rule of sub judice that prevents the Commons from interfering with the courts. With her commanding voice, she had an enviable control of the Commons, with famous yawns, "time's up", put-downs, and simply cutting off the microphone in the case of some. Her time in the chair met and exceeded all possible expectations.

Margo MacDonald (MP 1973–1974)

On 8th November 1973, Margo MacDonald won the Govan by-election for the SNP in a blaze of glory. Aged just 30, she woke your author (at the age of 13) up to the fact that women could become MPs. More astonishing than that was the fact that Govan was the "shipbuilding end" of Glasgow, which was a man's quarter in the very male-dominated "no mean city". She was blonde, beautiful, intelligent, and very feisty. Everyone was stunned! She failed to hold the seat in the next two general elections, but became Deputy leader of the SNP from 1974 to 1979. Her famous Govan victory presaged the election of 11 SNP MPs in 1974, with a third of Scottish voters choosing to support the party. This result rocked the British establishment to the core, at a time when the advent of the SNP as the natural party of government in a devolved Scotland could never have been imagined. It was she who urged the SNP to move to the left to win seats in Labour's heartlands. Her role was critical in enabling the SNP to move into government two decades later under Alex Salmond.

Margaret Beckett (MP 1974 – still incumbent)

Currently the longest-serving female MP in the House of Commons, first elected for Lincoln in 1974, she lost her seat in 1979, but won again for Derby South in 1983. She was the first woman deputy leader and acting leader of the Labour Party and Leader of the House, and when in government, she was the first woman President of the Board of Trade, Secretary of State for DEFRA, and Britain's first and only (to date) female Foreign Secretary.

As Leader of the House of Commons, she introduced Westminster Hall debates, which enable consensual cross-party discussion on matters not ordinarily discussed in the Chamber. In October 2006, as Foreign Secretary, she was the first to push through a major debate on climate change as a matter of peace and security. She argued that scientific evidence exceeded the worst fears about climate change, leading to migration on an unprecedented scale because of flooding, disease, and famine. This speech found its way into *21 Speeches that Shaped our World*[7]. She was a decade ahead of most British politicians who are only now just reluctantly acknowledging this, thanks to David Attenborough's *Blue Planet* series and the recent demonstrations by Extinction Rebellion.

It is the national minimum wage that provides Margaret with the greatest sense of pride. Whilst many claim it as their success, it was Margaret, as the Secretary of State for Trade and Industry, who dealt with the politics when arguments were had in Cabinet, legislative battles won in Parliament, and lives improved for millions of low-paid workers.

Harriet Harman (MP 1982 – still incumbent)
The longest continuously serving female MP and "Mother of the House", Harriet has held numerous ministerial and shadow ministerial positions, as well as being Solicitor General, Lord Privy Seal, and deputy and acting leader of the Labour Party. Whilst campaigning for deputy leadership, she had to take out a personal loan of £40k because out of all the contenders, she alone was unable to obtain backing from a union. Betrayed by both Tony Blair and Gordon Brown and vilified in the media for being "Harriet Harperson", she has battled on for the rights of women over the decades.

Harriet has achieved so many changes that have made life easier for women, including the 2010 Equalities Act, all-women shortlists, state-funded childcare, and the Domestic Violence Crime and Victims Act. Thanks to Harriet, women's representation and influence at all political levels has increased, working mothers have become the norm, women have progressed in business, and women's voices are heard throughout the realm. Harriet deserves, perhaps more than any other politician, her share of the credit for this and several Victoria Crosses for extreme valor against the massed male ranks against her.

Edwina Currie (MP 1983–1997)
A colourful and charismatic woman, as Under-Secretary of State in the Department of Health, she introduced nationwide

breast and cervical screening programmes for all women, making the UK the first country in the world to do so. This one measure has saved countless lives and has since been copied around the world. In 1994 she campaigned from the backbenches for equalizing the age of consent for all partners, whether straight, lesbian, or gay, which was groundbreaking. She also managed to reduce the age of consent for gay couples from 21 to 18.

Clare Short (MP 1983–2010)

Another fearless feminist, she fought hard against *The Sun* for its photos of topless women on Page 3. She tried twice to get through a Ten Minute Rule Bill, once sleeping all night outside the Clerk's Office, to be first in the queue. Sadly, both attempts ran out of debating time. *The Sun* carried out a vindictive media campaign afterwards to discredit her. Some of her best work was done as Minister for International Development, where she and her team promoted the new Millennium Development Goals from side issues into the nation's consciousness. Resigning three times from the front bench, she was an MP of principle, who finally resigned over the Iraq War, one of only two Labour MPs to do so.

Shirley Williams[8] (MP 1983–1974)

She graduated from Oxford with a degree in PPE Politics, Philosophy, and Economics and became Labour MP for Hitchin in 1964. In government, she quickly rose to a junior ministerial position, and between 1971 and 1973, she served as Shadow Home Secretary. In 1974, she became Secretary of State for Prices and Consumer Protection and then Secretary of State for Education and Paymaster General in 1976.

Whilst in office, she advocated for abolishing grammar schools and replacing them with the comprehensive school system. In

June 2012, she cited this as her greatest political achievement, stating: "I have never in any way regretted them and I still believe strongly in them".

She lost her seat in the 1979 election, though she remained a member of the National Executive Committee. In 1981, unhappy with the rising left-wing tide in the Labour Party, she resigned her membership to set up the new Social Democratic Party, along with Roy Jenkins David Owen, and Bill Rodgers, to become known as the "Gang of Four". She won the Crosby by-election later that year, becoming the first SDP MP.

Despite winning 25.4% of the popular vote in the 1983 general election, the SDP/Liberal Alliance only obtained 23 seats, in comparison to Labour, who got just 2% more at 27.6% of the popular vote but won 209 seats under our first past the post system. The Alliance came second again and again to the Conservatives across the country, since many perceived Labour as unfit to govern under the leadership of Michael Foot. Under a PR system, the Alliance would have held the balance of power, but instead the Conservatives won by a landslide. Shirley lost her seat and left the House of Commons. She moved to the USA in 1988 to serve as a Professor at Harvard before moving back to the UK in 1993, when she was made a life peer.

Mo Mowlam (MP 1987–2001)
It's fair to say that the Good Friday Agreement (which gave written form to the peace process in Northern Ireland and has held for 20 years) might never have been signed without Mo's contribution. She was a huge personality, possibly suffering from 'disinhibited behaviour' due to a long-growing brain tumour, from which she eventually died. This condition

59

enabled her to talk to anyone in a disinhibited manner, which endeared her to all.

Tessa Jowell (MP 1992–2015)
Tessa was passionate about helping babies and children born into poverty, working with young mothers, empowering women to provide a better future for themselves and their children, creating places and spaces to bring people together, and always looking for the practical difference that could be made. She was Secretary of State for Culture, Media, and Sport, Minister for Women, and Minister for the 2012 Olympics. She developed of the Sure Start scheme for young children, which brought together public health, parenting classes, and early years education to address disadvantage early in a child's life.

She also controversially introduced the 2005 Gambling Act, but the achievement for which she is most remembered is delivering a hugely successful 2012 Olympics in London. Sadly, she was diagnosed with a brain tumour in May 2017 and spent the remaining months of her life campaigning for other people with brain tumours for better research, diagnosis, and treatment. She was a hugely popular MP who united people from across the political spectrum.

Dame Margaret Hodge (MP 1994 – still incumbent)
A visionary Chair of the Islington Housing Committee, she ensured the Council bought up as much property as possible and also led a huge campaign to build new council housing. She was years ahead of her time in seeing the shortage of decent, affordable housing in the capital. After becoming an MP, she has become best known as Chair of the Public Accounts Committee, where she has become the scourge of HMRC and big business. She has scrutinised the small amounts

of corporation tax paid by some of the largest companies and challenged HMRC in the deals they have struck. As a result, the OECD took up the baton and international tax reporting rules changed within two years. A Jewish refugee born in Cairo, she has also been passionate about challenging anti-Semitism within the current Labour Party.

Jacqui Smith (MP 1997–2010)
The first female Home Secretary, she was only the third woman to hold one of the Great Offices of State. Her major achievements included the introduction of tougher prostitution laws, a reduction in crime rates, and the promotion of Police Community Support Officers. She introduced a crime-mapping scheme to allow citizens to access local crime information and she managed to pass the 42-day detention law plans. She also announced the introduction of a national ID card project in 2009, but this was later thrown out by the Lib Dem–Conservative coalition in 2010 on grounds of cost. She refused to downgrade ecstasy from a class A drug and returned cannabis to the status of class B drug.

Theresa May (MP 1997 – still incumbent)
Theresa is only the second woman to be Prime Minister of the UK. She was first female Chair of the Conservative Party and famously told them at their party conference in 2002 that they must try to change their image of being the "nasty party". The longest-lived Home Secretary for over 60 years, she was only the fourth woman to hold one of the Great Offices of State. She abolished Labour's National ID card scheme and reformed the regulations on the retention of DNA samples and the use of CCTV cameras. She introduced the "snooper's charter" and announced radical cuts to the police force. She later criticized the Police Federation for their culture and abolished ASBOs.

She introduced anti-immigrant legislation, pledging to bring immigration down to below 100,000, and presided over a number of well-publicised deportation decisions, Abu Qatada being the most notorious. Her "go home or face arrest" advertisements were widely criticized, as was the Windrush scandal. She was also briefly the Minister for Women and Equalities. She became Prime Minister shortly after David Cameron resigned in June 2016 in the wake of the Brexit vote.

However, her tenure was dominated by Brexit: though she attempted to get "her Brexit deal" through Parliament three times, it was voted down each time. She was widely criticized for her refusal to compromise or build cross-party collaborations, although at the same time the British public admired her for battling on with a job that no-one at the time wanted. Towards the end, she looked an exhausted and betrayed figure, with many ordinary people remarking "please put her out of her misery". She eventually agreed to stand down as Prime Minister on 7th June 2019, immediately after the D-Day celebrations and Donald Trump's visit.

Jo Cox[9] (MP 2015–2016)

She studied Social and Political Sciences at Cambridge. She worked first as a political assistant and then joined Oxfam in 2001, where she became Head of Policy and Advocacy by 2005. She was selected to contest the Batley and Spen parliamentary seat in 2015, after the previous incumbent, Mike Wood, decided not to stand.

She held the seat for Labour, with an increased majority, and became a campaigner on issues relating to the Syrian Civil War and founded and chaired the All Party Parliamentary Group: Friends of Syria. Despite being tiny, she fought passionately for her causes, which also included the Labour Friends of Palestine and the Middle East, and she called for the lifting of the blockade of the Gaza Strip.

Tragically, on 16th June 2016, barely a week before the referendum on membership of the EU, she died after being shot and stabbed multiple times in Birstall, where she had been due to hold a constituency surgery. Thomas Mair was found guilty of her murder in November and sentenced to life imprisonment with a whole life order. She was a secular humanist and left behind a husband and two young children, aged five and three.

So, why do women go into politics today?

Anne Milton trained as a nurse at St Bart's Hospital. After qualifying, she worked in the NHS for 25 years and was also a shop steward for the Royal College of Nursing. She was a Councillor for Reigate and Banstead from 1994 to 2004. She stood as the Conservative candidate for Guildford in the 2005 general election and won by a very small margin of 347 votes. After taking her seat, she was made a member of the Health and Social Care Committee.

"Why did I go into politics? I didn't think people like me were represented very well. It was a whim. It was a 'gosh, you know, I quite fancy being an MP'. I was making supper, steak and kidney pie, I remember the evening! And serendipity, I went shopping with my sister that week and there was a lifestyle magazine, I've still got the article, written by a Conservative candidate that said: 'how to become an MP'. It was just quite extraordinary. That was my greatest achievement, getting here, because most people have got a contact in politics or have met somebody. But I started out from scratch, a self-made politician, I watched people making speeches and thinking what was good, what was bad, learning it from first principles really".

"And winning the Guildford seat was the three hardest years of my life. We didn't hold the seat, so I had to win it off the opposition. It wasn't a Conservative seat, it wasn't a safe seat, far from it, it had been lost in 2001. I had tried to get a seat in the 2001 election, and wasn't successful, though I did quite well. I got down to the final in three seats, so that was quite good. I had never fought a seat before. We had lost the seat in 2001 and it took three years to win it back, so that was hard, but I've increased my majority since then".

Anneliese Dodds: "I first got interested in political issues when I was at school. I had a job as a kitchen porter and I was paid £2 an hour, so it was before the minimum wage came in. I had a lot of friends who were older than me, well, adults, who were doing that job basically as their career, and it seemed to be unfair it was so low paid and they were struggling, so that got me politicized. Then when I went to university (Oxford), I joined the Labour Club and got involved at that stage. I held office in the Party, though I did it in parallel with my academic work. I did a PhD and was planning to focus on my academic career, when we were told to put people's names down for the EU elections and my partner suggested I should apply".

"Initially I thought 'oh no, I can't do that, not sure I was capable'; I was also pregnant, so I thought 'oh, I don't know, this is too hard', but then my partner said I was always complaining and how unhappy I was about media coverage of the EU, so I thought 'yes, fair enough' and I ended up at the top of the list and was selected as an MEP for three years".

"Then we had the snap general election, which was a big surprise to me, and my existing MP, Andrew Smith, was standing down. He'd been incumbent for 30 years. I knew him very well, and when I heard he was standing down, a number of people said they hoped I would think of standing. It's where I live and I really love Oxford, and I thought 'yes, I would like to do this', and that was how it happened. And most importantly, the people of Oxford East were willing to vote for me. That was the best thing, and I'm very grateful to them for it".

Heidi Allen had worked in business all her life, in very male-dominated industries, including ExxonMobil and Royal Mail, before joining the family paint business set up by her parents and now run by her husband. She was inspired to get into politics after watching the scenes from the 2011 Tottenham riots.

She first became a councillor in St Albans for 18 months before trying to become an MP. Her first attempt, for South East Cambridgeshire, ended in disappointment. There was a counting error of 23 votes, which would have given Heidi the seat, but the error was only discovered after the counting officer had gone home, so it was null and void. She then tried for South Cambridgeshire in 2015 and won with 51% of the vote, increasing the Tory majority.

"It was the Tottenham riots in 2011, it just shook me out of my comfort zone, I thought my country was falling apart. I love a mess! If I see a mess, I love to just get in there and try and tidy it, and it kind of felt like that. And I didn't know how you did it, how you became an MP. I just used Google and learnt everything from that".

"It just shows that you don't have to be, you know, 'your father was a peer,' and all of this rubbish. You can just do it from a standing start. That's pretty amazing really, that we have this democratic system, where if you want to, you don't need any particular qualifications, you don't need to be educated or wealthy or have connections. You just have to do your research. You don't know the right people, but get to know the right people and it's perfectly possible. I think that's quite encouraging for people that wouldn't have thought about doing it otherwise".

Dr Sarah Wollaston was born in Woking and studied medicine at Guy's Hospital in London. She qualified in 1986 and worked as a junior hospital doctor and then a GP. After over 20 years of clinical practice, she ran for political office. She was the first person to be selected as a Parliamentary candidate through a postal open primary. During the campaign, she emphasized that she was not a career politician and had actually had a real job. She became Conservative MP for Totnes in the 2010 General Election with an increased majority, which she further increased in 2015. At the time of writing, she is Chair of the Health Select Committee.

On 20th February 2019 Sarah resigned from the Conservative Party, along with Heidi Allen and Anna Soubry, over the Party's stance on Brexit and all three joined the Independent Group, later renamed Change UK, with Heidi Allen being appointed interim leader. In June 2019 she and Heidi quit that party to sit as Independent MPs. Sarah joined the Liberal Democrats on 14th August and Heidi joined them on 7th October 2019.

"I had never been interested in politics. I'd never been to a political meeting in my life. I had had a career in medicine for 24 years, teaching and training junior doctors, and then I heard

David Cameron saying on TV that they needed more people who'd come from other backgrounds, other than politics, to stand for Parliament. 'We need women', and it was a direct personal call to say: 'don't think you can't do it, if you want to apply, then apply', and so I did. And I think that's an example of how, actually, you have to deal with a pipeline issue, because it's that sense of imposter syndrome that I still have even though I'm here…am I the right person? Am I good enough? That's the kind of question we all have. The impact of someone directly sending out a message saying: 'we want you to apply', can be very powerful".

"I spend a lot of my time speaking at meetings, and I will often say to people, as I did a fortnight ago when I spoke to a group of NHS clinical leaders, and I'll suggest they apply for my job, and then I'll follow it up with: 'you can send me an email if you're interested'. I met with somebody who followed up from that meeting, who had worked in the NHS all her life and she said: 'you know what, I'd like to run for Parliament, but I don't know how to do it'".

"It's not just that point about having the high-level messages that David Cameron put out, but also that individual point of contact and being prepared to follow it up to meet with people who then take you up on the offer. Because so many women across all political parties have been in that position, and I've said to them: 'why don't you apply' and get them, because it's the pipeline issue more than anything else that we need to address. We need to get people to consider applying for the job, because otherwise, we're always going to struggle".

The wisdom is that women have to be asked three times to apply for a job, whilst men only have to be asked once.

The pipeline issue is that out of ten PPC candidates, nine of them will be men and only one a woman. In that instance, her chances of getting selected are virtually zero.

"I did have an interesting experience when I applied. I went to see the agent, who looked me up and down and said: 'you don't stand a gnat's chance in hell, but we do need a few more women on the shortlist!' She was trying to be kind, because she was worried I'd be wasting my time and wouldn't get a safe seat and she wanted me to know that it wasn't going to be a piece of cake. She wanted me to be realistic about the challenges ahead. And I do the same, not in those terms, but I do point out that it's a tough job and there are a lot of hurdles to cross, so people need to go into it with their eyes open, but in a way that doesn't put them off applying. So it's about being realistic, and encouraging them at the same time".

Jess Phillips is the youngest of four children. Her father, Stewart Trainor, was a teacher, whilst her mother, Jean Trainor, was Deputy Chief Executive of the NHS Confederation and Chair of South Birmingham Mental Health Trust. They were politically active: "Growing up with my father was like growing up with Jeremy Corbyn", she told Rachel Cooke of *The Observer*[10] in March 2016. Jess went to King Edward VI Camp Hill School for Girls, a local grammar school. Her childhood ambition was to become Prime Minister.

Jess studied Economic and Social History at the University of Leeds and marched in protest against the Iraq War. From 2010 onwards, she worked in Women's Aid and had a post as a business development manager, responsible for refugees from sexual abuse in the West Midlands. Jess left the Labour Party during the years of Tony Blair's leadership and rejoined after the 2010 election. Her period at Women's Aid made Phillips "utterly pragmatic...I learned that my principles don't matter as much as people's lives". She was elected as a Labour Councillor in 2010 and was then appointed as the victims' champion at Birmingham City Council, lobbying police and criminal justice associations on behalf of victims. She also served on the West Midlands Police and Crime Panel before being elected as MP for Birmingham Yardley in 2015.

"I've been involved in politics all my life. My parents, before I was born, they were the people who ran election-day activities from our house. We were always campaigning about something. The Labour Party was like our family. It was everything, everybody I grew up with. I went to Women's Liberation Play Group. Everybody I grew up with was in the Labour Party, so politics is in my blood. But I decided to try and do something, become an elected representative when I was working for Women's Aid and I saw how bad policy decisions were at the local council and at the national level. Some very poor policy decisions were made by people who didn't know what they were talking about. So, I thought that I had better get involved and do something about it".

"I had no role models, I didn't have any political pin-ups or anything like that. My mum was an activist for big campaigns, whether that was against big drug companies or in her job working in the health service. My mum and nan were both real political activists and would change things by proper protest".

Lisa Cameron is an SNP politician and a clinical psychologist. She was born in Glasgow and grew up in East Kilbride. She obtained a BSc in Psychology from the University of Strathclyde, an MSc in Psychology from the University of Stirling, and a doctorate in Clinical Psychology from the University of Glasgow. She worked as a clinical psychologist for the NHS before entering politics. She was first elected in 2015 as MP for East Kilbride, Strathaven, and Lesmahagow. She voted in favour of Scottish independence in the 2014 Scottish Referendum. "I worked as a psychologist for over 20 years in mental health and many of the issues that people started to come and speak to me about, linked to mental health, were more social austerity issues, linked to financial problems, housing, things that affect mental health, but that you can't impact through therapy because it's about situational change".

"So I decided to get involved in politics to support people and mental health. I'm glad to be the spokesperson on mental health in the party, to champion the issues that I think are important. But I also felt that with my background, if I entered politics, I could change policies to help people".

"There was no politics in my family. At the time I got involved, I hadn't been in politics before, but I had been a union rep for 14 years in the NHS. So that was probably the first step towards getting involved in politics, since I was advocating for people and helping them with their issues. I was looking at legislation and employment law in the NHS, and negotiating and speaking up at meetings and representing people, so rather than having a parental background in it, I had a professional link via my job".

Caroline Spelman: "I was working in industry and it had never occurred to me at all to be a politician, but I felt uncomfortable when I discovered the sugar industry was exporting its surplus sugar onto the market with a subsidy. That had the effect of crashing the price for farmers in developing countries. And I felt that was wrong. It is very difficult to persuade an industry that has become dependent on things like subsidy to voluntarily give up on it. So I realized that if I was going to change that situation, which I thought was iniquitous, I'd have to become a legislator".

"So, it took time, it took about ten years to get into politics. But I campaigned.... I suppose it's the trade justice issue that drove me and there are now no export subsidies on sugar from the EU. In fact, trade justice and fair trade has become quite common parlance. I spoke to a school group yesterday and they all asked me the same question: how did you get into politics? And I said: 'I'll bet you all like Fair Trade chocolate?', and there were lots of nods, and they know what it is. We forget that 30 years ago, people didn't talk about that sort of thing. Trade justice brought me in, and it's fairly typical for politicians to see something that needs putting right and then get involved".

Final thoughts
It is interesting to note from this brief review of female MPs over the last hundred years, that many were well ahead of their time, discussing uncomfortable subjects (for male MPs) such as FGM, domestic violence, sex trafficking, equal pay, and child marriage. Aside from female-specific issues, they were also passionate about social welfare and animal and climate issues.

Sadly, most were unable to make as much change to legislation as they would have liked, simply because they didn't get the support from a majority male House of Commons, which was more interested in discussing war, defence, munitions, banking, roads, railways, and construction. Of course, all of these issues are important, but "male issues" have had too much discussion, whilst "female issues" have had too little over the previous two hundred years of Parliament.

More progress is being made today because there are sufficient numbers of female MPs to give support and a hearing to those who speak out on "female issues", which, let's not forget, are human issues which have knock-on effects on children, partners, and business.

Much thanks is given to Iain Dale and Jacqui Smith for compiling two impressive volumes of *The Honourable* Ladies,[11] which devotes a brief essay to every female MP who has ever been elected. Many have been written out of history, or in fact were never written *into* history. Many of these earlier female MPs have no written biography and tiny mentions in Wikipedia; a sad fact remains that only 9% of the content of Wikipedia is about women.[12]

References:

1.Wikipedia (2018) [online]. Available at: https://en.wikipedia.org/wiki/Constance_Markievicz [accessed 10th Feb 2019].

2. Wikipedia (2018) [online]. Available at: https://en.wikipedia.org/wiki/Nancy_Astor,_Viscountess_Astor [accessed 12th Jan 2019].

3. Wikipedia (2018) [online]. Available at: https://en.wikipedia.org/wiki/Margaret_Bondfield [accessed 14th Feb 2019].

4. Wikipedia (2018) [online]. Available at: https://en.wikipedia.org/wiki/Ellen_Wilkinson [accessed 12th Feb 2019].

5. Wikipedia (2018) [online]. Available at:
https://en.wikipedia.org/wiki/Barbara_Castle
[accessed 15th Feb 2019].

6. Wikipedia (2018) [online]. Available at:
https://en.wikipedia.org/wiki/Margaret_Thatcher
[accessed 3rd Mar 2019].

7. Abbott, C. (2010). *21 Speeches that Shaped Our World*.
London. Random House.

8. Wikipedia (2018) [online]. Available at:
https://en.wikipedia.org/wiki/Shirley_Williams
[accessed 10th Jan 2019].

9. Wikipedia (2018) [online]. Available at:
https://en.wikipedia.org/wiki/Jo_Cox
[accessed 20th Mar 2019].

10. *The Guardian* (2016) [online]. Available at:
https://www.theguardian.com/politics/2016/mar/06/jess-
phillips-someone-to-believe-in
[accessed 17th Jan 2019].

11. Dale, I. and Smith, J. (2018). *The Honourable Ladies Volume 1*. London: Biteback Publishing.

12. Wikipedia (2018) [online]. Available at:
https://en.wikipedia.org/wiki/Gender_bias_on_Wikipedia
[accessed 15th May 2019].

Chapter 3

Do women do politics differently?

Does gender really matter that much? Across the world, women have a harder time getting elected in the first place, and even after being elected, they have a harder job getting re-elected. As a result of both of these factors, they work a lot harder in office to serve their constituents[1].

Research undertaken in the USA (but which could equally apply to any other country around the globe) shows that when women run for office, the media treats them differently. Women don't get as much coverage as men, and when they do, the focus is often on "soft" issues, such as their appearance and families. Simply adding information about a candidate's appearance has been found to decrease the likelihood of people voting in their favour.

Female candidates often face well-funded and high-quality male opponents. Typically, a strong male challenger who enters a race will deter other challengers from running or will "clear the field". However, when a woman enters a race, even if she is a strong candidate, or often *because* she is, other (male) candidates will persist in running against her. Female incumbents are similarly more likely to face stronger challengers than their male counterparts.

Women must also contend with voters who hold gender stereotypes and interest groups or potential donors who often don't hold female candidates in high regard. Some voters explicitly prefer male candidates, even when evidence shows that the female candidate is better qualified. Donald Trump is a good example here. Survey data also shows that 39% of the US population explicitly prefers a majority male government,

74

as opposed to only 9% who might prefer a majority female government.

Are women better representatives?

Evidence from *Gendered Vulnerability*, a book by Jeffrey Lazarus and Amy Steigerwalt,[2] shows that congresswomen spend more time and effort communicating with their constituents. Congresswomen send out 17% more mail to constituents than Congressmen, and they deliver more government spending to their constituencies. Congresswomen direct anywhere between 20% and 100% more spending to their voters, and they also appoint 3.5 more staff members in their states than Congressmen.

Congresswomen more closely represent their constituents' interests, and they also introduce more bills related to policy areas that are important to their constituents. They are also more likely to vote in ways that reflect their constituents' needs. Electing more women isn't just about identity politics, though of course women do make up 51% of the population; it's also about ensuring women's issues are better discussed and acted upon and that there is a "female take" on legislation being created or amended.

Do women and men have different leadership styles?

A World Economic Forum[3] report on female leadership style says that female leadership is often associated with issues such as health, sexual violence, gender gaps in employment, better education, and financial inclusion. UN Women's executive director Phumzile Mlambo-Ngcuka observes: "Where there are more women in decision-making positions, we see more inclusive decisions, and we find different solutions to long-standing problems". But the record on female political leadership (like that of men) is mixed. For example, Argentina's

Cristina Fernandez de Kirchner helped to narrow the country's gender poverty gap, but she also imposed a ban on abortions and defaulted on international loan payments.

Brazil's Dilma Rousseff appointed record numbers of women to higher office, including cabinet positions, but her presidency ended with an embattled economy and allegations of corruption. Female political leaders have engaged in conflicts and traded arms to nations repressive of women's rights. Margaret Thatcher engaged in the Falklands War and presided over the UK selling many arms to Saudi Arabia. She cut the number of people working in the Equal Opportunities Commission, did not support state-funded childcare, and had only one woman in her Cabinet.

Many people in the UK might have thought that Theresa May's leadership was lacking with regard to Brexit, though she was being sabotaged by men on both sides and picked up a job that no-one else wanted at the time. Like many women before her, she was set up to fail. History shows that only when a country of company is in crisis do women get appointed almost out of desperation and then they have a far higher chance of failing. Theresa had fewer women (4/23) in her cabinet than David Cameron, but she was a true feminist, promoting legislation like the anti-modern slavery Bill whilst Home Secretary and she set up the Women2Win campaign back in 2005 which has made a massive difference to improving the numbers of women in the Conservative Party since then. Had she been able to stay in power longer, and get past Brexit she may well have introduced a lot more female friendly legislation and it's a tragedy that she didn't have the time to do this.

Angela Merkel, dubbed the most powerful woman in the world and Germany's Iron Chancellor since 2005, has been bossing

European male leaders around for the last 14 years. Like Margaret Thatcher, she did nothing for the feminist cause for many years, but finally, in 2015, she made an announcement ahead of the G7 summit that she wanted to devote time to discussing the improvement of women's lot in the workplace and also set targets for women on company boards. It is interesting that it was only after a decade in power and once she was comfortably ensconced in her position of power that she felt strong enough to finally devote some time to the sisterly cause.

Political leadership does not operate in a vacuum
Women's political leadership continues to be diverted by the notion that 'women's issues' somehow diverge from other policy issues, and equally that other policy issues are somehow not 'women's issues'. There is also a disregard for the institutional and countrywide culture within which all leaders have to operate.

Rethinking 'women's issues'
Women's issues tend to cover topics like: wage equality, childcare provision, reproductive rights, girls' education, violence against women, healthcare, and representation in politics and business. History shows that not all female leaders advance these issues. Two women prime ministers of Bangladesh, Khaleda Zia and Sheikh Hasina, made little to no effort to advance women's rights between 1991 and 2006. History also shows that successful political leadership involves more than promoting women's issues at the expense of others. A successful leader should champion causes that advance a society overall. Of course, this will include all women's causes, but perhaps, to gain traction, these causes should be sold to voters as beneficial to the entire society, not just to women.

Matters of national security, tax reform, trade and economic policies, technology regulation, energy policies, criminal justice reform – these directly and significantly affect women around the world. Equally, including women in national financial systems has been shown to drive sustainable economic growth. Educating girls brings long-term gains in national living standards and better education of their children when they become mothers. All of these issues are not just 'women's issues', but are sensible economic and social policies for the advancement of society in general.

Institutions and national culture vs. individuals

Debates over women's political leadership also tend to subscribe to the idea of individual over institution. They hinge on the Weberian notion of leadership, which relies on an individual's distinctiveness making her uniquely able to lead. What is often most noted about Margaret Thatcher, Angela Merkel, Hilary Clinton, and other female leaders is their gender, which seems to matter more than the institutions to which they belong.

However, like their male colleagues, the political actions of female leaders are institutionally constrained. These constraints are formal (rules, laws, and procedures) and informal (institutional cultures and norms). Kersti Kaljulaid is Estonia's youngest and first female President, and she has made huge progress in advancing her country towards an inclusive, digital society. But violence against women is still a big challenge in Estonia and the country's gender pay gap is amongst the highest in Europe. Leadership matters, but often institutions matter more, and one embattled female leader can only achieve so much against ingrained institutional and cultural gender bias. By overestimating the clout of female leadership, we underestimate the importance of its contextual settings.

So, the cultural climate of the state is more critical to the success of 'women's issues' than the number of women in power. However, you can argue that as the number of women in power increases, the cultural setting will change, as we have seen in Westminster. Hillary Clinton was able to achieve far less for women in the USA because the percentage of women in the Senate and in Congress is much lower than in the UK. Even if she had become President, it seems unlikely that she could have brought in state-funded maternity leave, abortion on demand, or any kind of state-provided childcare, because the culture in America is far more macho, religion is far stronger, and there is an aversion to state spending on any sort of family support. Look at how Obama had to battle for years just to improve access to healthcare.

Any state must have the political commitment and ability to challenge long-held gendered and cultural norms in order to create change. This is a structural feature separate from the identity of any particular leader or party. Any state must be democratic, insofar as it allows for a well-developed civil society able to discuss and support women's rights. So, progress with 'women's issues' and on women's political effectiveness needs to focus on the institutions and the reforms they must also undertake, not just on the leaders or MPs. The time for female political leadership has come, but we must rethink how we judge this leadership and what else must be done to ensure its success. It is ironic that just as women are entering politics in greater numbers around the globe, populations are becoming increasingly disenchanted with how broken most political systems appear to be. Perhaps some farsighted women can play a much larger role in cleaning up politics worldwide.

Rosie Duffield became the first ever Labour MP for Canterbury in the June 2017 election. A single mother of two boys aged 14 and 16 and a former teaching assistant dependent on tax credits, she campaigned tirelessly against the 30-year Tory incumbent Sir Julian Brazier, a 63-year-old knight of the realm and a staunch Brexiteer. Every night, she would come home exhausted from trailing the streets, knocking on doors, and speaking to countless people.

However, against all the odds, she won by 187 votes out of over 50,000 cast. Canterbury had the record for being the longest-held seat by any one party, having been Tory since its creation in 1918. A good-looking young blonde mother, intelligent and articulate, Rosie became an overnight media sensation.

Labour had such little hope of ever getting an MP that it had no office in Canterbury, and Rosie was obliged to ask Labour HQ for financial help to acquire an office since she had no savings or recourse to other finances. Described as "a wolf in sheep's clothing" by her mother and regularly asked questions like "did you ever think you could win?", "when are you getting married?", and "how do you get the glitter in your hair?", she is now completely loving her job. Full of positivity and enthusiasm, there is a sparkle in her eye, which would inspire anyone considering entering Parliament.

Rosie is a big supporter of the 50:50 in Parliament[4] and #AskHerToStand campaigns set up by Frances Scott. She has hosted a number of events in Parliament to encourage other ordinary women to try and become MPs.

So, do women do politics differently?
Rosie: "I don't want to be sexist, but I'm going to say yes, because traditionally our time has been so limited. Because we are split between all of the things we do, we just get on with things. We don't want to spend hours and hours mulling over things, delaying everything, we just want to get on with it".

"People say to me all the time, why can't you [politicians] work together? Cross-party on health, why can't we? Obviously the nature of party politics is that you don't do that, but at the same time, there are lots of areas where you can. And actually, there is now lots of cross-party co-operation and I am really pleased to see that. I've spent lots of time chatting to women on the other side, and politics doesn't really come into it. We just have to do the best we can for our constituents. So, I think women do work more collaboratively, actually. You know, not always because we're talking about people and people are different, but I think we have a more joined-up vision if possible".

Heidi Allen: "Yes, without a doubt, I think we are more collaborative in talking, not so much testosterone there. That's not to say it can't get heated in the Chamber with women, it can, but I think we're more interested in solutions than 'it was my idea'. If the solution is right, I am happy. I'm not happy just because I thought of it. And that builds a more collaborative, solution-focused way of working, rather than just testosterone and power games: 'I'm right and you're wrong'".

"Regarding the refurbishment of Parliament, the whole debate at the moment is whether they do it whilst we're here or we all get shipped out. I'm very pragmatic: it's a place of work, it's a building. Yes, architecturally of course it needs preserving, because it's a part of British history. But do I care if we don't move back here, or [if we] end up in some purpose-built modern debating chamber somewhere? Then the latter would suit me just fine. I refuse to be overawed by the building here. It's just a place of work. There are some who call me all sorts of unmentionable names for that and who worry that if we move out, we will never move back. I think we should do whatever is cheaper. It's the public purse".

Kate Green worked for Barclays Bank for 15 years, followed by a two-year secondment to the Home Office. She was then Director of the National Council for One Parent Families and after this became CEO of the Child Poverty Action Group. She stood unsuccessfully for the 1997 General Election as the Labour candidate for the Cities of London and Westminster in the 1997 general election and finally succeeded in 2010, when she became the Labour MP for Stretford and Urmston. In 2011, Kate was promoted to Shadow Minister of State for Equalities at the Government Equalities Office, working alongside Yvette Cooper.

In February 2012, Kate complained about a beer sold in the House of Commons Stranger's Bar called "Top Totty" that depicted the image of a bikini-clad bunny girl on the beer pump handle, which she said was demeaning to women. The Leader of the House, Sir George Young, upheld her complaint and had the beer removed.

Kate: "Yes, up to a point, women do politics differently. I'm on a whole lot of WhatsApp groups, one of which is an all-women's group, and the conversations on that group are very different from the others. The others are very functional: we're having this meeting at this time or we're signing this amendment, or are we happy with what we've just heard in the Chamber? Whilst the all-women's WhatApp group is very different, it's very supportive, it's 'happy birthday and you were brilliant on the Today programme this morning' and 'it's outrageous the way the Tories treated you in the Chamber'. There is good factual stuff in there too, but there's all this sisterly support going on that doesn't exist in the other groups. So, amongst ourselves, I think we do politics very differently, even in my own party".

"But externally, in the Chamber? No, I don't think we do. Men and women behave pretty similarly, as in we're all different, some are more collaborative, some are more confrontational or analytical or whatever, and I don't think that divides on gender lines. But subjects we take an interest in: I think it's sad that more women are likely to be specializing in *soft social* subjects, to characterize them in a rather derogatory manner, rather than hard, economic, foreign policy, defence, economy, or those sort of areas. If you look at the debates that men and women participate in, in the Commons, you would see women are more active in debates on areas like health, social care, and families and less active than men in the debates on money, defence, and foreign affairs".

Anne Milton: "Yes, women do politics differently, they tend to be more consensual. They look for agreement, not difference, I think that they look for solutions".

"In John Cleese's book: *Families and How to Survive Them*, he draws the distinction that little boys growing up try to define themselves by differences with their mothers. So, they separate from their mothers, whereas little girls tend to get close to their mothers, and I think that's played out in politics too. Girls tend to come together, to work something out, whereas boys tend to pride themselves on their distance. So I think boys instinctively go for a more adversarial way of working than girls do in politics, which, in a sense, is 'us against them'. I don't think women have that need to draw out the differences".

Chi Onwurah's maternal grandfather was a sheet metal worker in the Tyneside dockyards during the great depression of the 1930s. Her mother grew up in poverty in Garth Heads on Tyneside's Quayside. Her father, from Nigeria, was working as a dentist when they met and married in the 1950s.

After Chi was born in Wallsend, Newcastle, her family moved to Nigeria in 1965 when she was still a baby. Just two years later, the Biafra war broke out, forcing her mother to return to Newcastle whilst Chi's father remained in the Biafran Army. Chi graduated from Imperial College in 1987 with a degree in electrical engineering. She worked in hardware and software development in mainly private sector companies in a number of different countries.

Prior to entering Parliament, Chi was Head of Telecoms at OfCOM, and she was also active in the Anti-Apartheid Movement, spending many years on its national executive committee.

"Politics is different when women are there. I'm against generalizing about what women do, because there is always more difference within a group than between groups. It's always this basic behavioural thing, but when there are more women in politics and in the room, the room is different, there is less testosterone, and it's more balanced".

"The Chamber, as I understand it, I mean, I wasn't here, when women made up only like 3% of MPs back in 1983, but Harriet Harman tells me that the Chamber today, even though it is far from balanced, is much better than it was, so that has changed".

Jo Swinson: "Yes, it is a sweeping generalization, and there's more variety between how different women and men do politics than between men and women as a whole, but there are some differences, and I notice that when the House of Commons, on the rare occasion when there are more women than men in there, on dates like celebrating the centenary of women's suffrage or in debates like stuff on sexual harassment, there are a few occasions when you get more women than men in the Chamber, and it does feel different".

"That is quite a generalization, so you get women who hector and shout others down with the best of them, and you get many men who are thoughtful and listen to different points of view. But there are some differences: women are often more cooperative with others, so it's more about working collectively, and this may be because there is a shared appreciation of being the underdog, and cross-party working is often easier with women MPs, because there's an underlying bond of solidarity, but as I say, women do it differently, men do it differently, as individuals, and we shouldn't stereotype and suggest that to be a woman politician you have to do it like a, b, or c, and ditto for men".

Lisa Cameron: "I think women would like to do politics differently. They are pushed into behaving in a more adversarial and masculine way than they would normally, particularly when they are leading parties, and I think women who come into Parliament don't have the network initially of the old boys' club that exists here. So they have to do things differently because a lot of decisions seem to be made through who you know and how long you've known them rather than what you know".

"It is a shame that women try to emulate male MP's styles to get to the top, because we have other skills that are just as valuable but haven't been seen as leadership skills politically. But they are important skills, so women do manage things differently, but some try to behave more masculinely. The other thing is about having to do things differently because we don't necessarily come into these networks".

"Are things different for Scottish MPs? No, I feel that MPs who have been here quite some time have established networks. People that they know very well, that they know who to go to, if they need something to shift. It takes a long time to establish that. But there's also perhaps more in the Conservative Party than in the others. There's also these networks of people having gone to school together, having gone through the same sort of background, and having a long history together; they've been to university together and have those connections in Parliament".

References:

1. The World Economic Forum. (2018). [online]. Available at: https://www.weforum.org/agenda/2018/03/why-you-should-vote-for-a-woman-in-2018/
[accessed 7th November 2018]

2. Lazarus, J. and Steigerwalt, A. (2018). *Gendered Vulnerability*. Michigan. Michigan Publishing.

3. The World Economic Forum. (2018). [online]. Available at: https://www.weforum.org/agenda/2018/12/do-men-and-women-have-different-leadership-styles/
[accessed 10th October 2018]

4. 50:50 Parliament. (2018). [online]. Available at: https://5050parliament.co.uk/ and #AskHertoStand
[accessed 3rd March 2019]

Chapter 4

"Physical fitness and health" – Kate Green

"You need to be OK with people hating you" – Jess Phillips

"Passion, resilience and a bit of a thick skin" – Heidi Allen

Skills benefitting an MP

Have confidence
Women constantly doubt their abilities. The old adage says that women need to be asked to do a job three times before they will consider it, whereas men don't wait to be asked, they just go ahead and do it.

Women also wait until they are super- or over-qualified for a job; they want a 90% fit with the job specification, whereas many men will apply for a job with barely a 50% fit. And considering the role of MP has no job specification, that in itself is ironically another barrier to women, since they have nothing to tick their skills off against. Women are much less likely to leap into the unknown.

Even when women have equal rights, they don't take the same opportunities as men.

This is due to stereotyped behaviour taught to girls from virtually the day they are born, not to be pushy, to put others first, to wait and be asked or told, to behave, to be good, and not to argue or answer back. Just being told to put your hand up at school and wait to be asked creates a passive approach to life and one that teachers should be more aware of. Whilst girls dutifully raise their hands in class and wait to be asked, they often aren't because the boys have already shouted out the answer.

Research shows that in mixed schools, boys get about 65% of teachers' attention. The depressing YouTube video "Run Like a Girl"[1] shows that young girls aged ten will run properly, but when teenage girls are asked to run like a girl, they stage a stupid run with flapping arms and an ungainly gait. Some serious negative stereotyping has happened in those years around puberty. This is the 21st century with supposed equality for girls and women, but society is not teaching them this. Focusing on girls' looks from day one of their lives does not help.

We are now living in an ever more visual society, where images of beautiful, perfect women assail us from every medium: no wonder girls' and women's corresponding happiness is falling through the floor. Recent research on teenage girls in the UK showed that 25% of them were unhappy with their bodies and had undertaken self-harm in the past year.[2] The number of women having breast enlargements and uplifts (as distinct from reconstructive surgery after breast cancer) has been rising by about 4% year on year since the 1990s, to over 420,000 operations[3] on women in the USA in the last year. The ubiquitous availability of online porn only cements the idea that women's bodies and faces should be perfect.

We can all make an effort not to describe a young baby girl in terms of her looks. Rather than saying how beautiful she is, say "what a clever little thing she is, she's already recognized me/my voice/her toy, etc". Ask yourself "would I describe a boy like this?" If not, then it's not helpful for a girl either. Don't make beauty platitudes just to please the parents. And tell them why. It's lazy to just comment on appearance without digging deeper.

Several of the MPs interviewed for this book, even a former minister (Sarah Wollaston), said they often experienced imposter syndrome, where they thought "am I good enough?", "why am I in this job?", "isn't there someone better?" If men think this, they certainly don't admit to it.

Like people, problem-solving and listening skills
Anne Milton: "You need to like people, warts and all. You need to like people with different views from yourself, like people who are cross, angry, happy, sad, desperate....

You also need to be good at problem-solving. Somebody comes to see you with a problem, and you need to work out what's the best way of solving it. You need to be able to prioritise your day and your work, so deciding when you do what. You'll enjoy it more if you're good at managing your time well. You need quite a lot of experience to do the job and you need experience of life and to be emotionally intelligent".

Anticipating how the media may report a story
It helps if you can anticipate how the media might report a story. Anne Milton remembers doing a speech at the Royal College of Nurses annual conference – which took place in the middle of a controversial piece of legislation, so it was a potentially angry audience – and she remembers a woman asking her: "I don't want to ask about the legislation coming through, I want to ask you about what it's like being an MP as a second career".

So Anne relaxed into this question and said: "It's great as a second job, because the thing is, when you're over 40, you know lots of things that you didn't know before". The headline in three national newspapers the next day, because it was in the heat of the health plan debate, was "Anne Milton, Health Minister, says David Cameron and Nick Clegg are too young for politics!"

Could Anne have anticipated the angle the media would take? Probably not; you'd need to have a crystal ball to do that calculation in your head before replying. And perhaps that is what many senior politicians are trying to do too much of these days, hence their non-answers to many questions, which frustrates the public. We prefer real people like Jess Phillips and Nigel Farage, who give honest rather than calculated answers.

Don't be seduced by the media
As Isabel Hardman pointed out in her book *Why We Get the Wrong Politicians*, as a journalist, she never had any problem getting time with an MP. She quoted several MPs as being happy to spend 30 minutes with her having a coffee then rushing off to a vote admitting they had no idea what they were voting on. One can easily argue that they should have forgone the 30-minute coffee with her so they would have had some time to prepare for the vote. But sadly, there is little reward for diligent MPs spending time on scrutinizing bills or legislation, since their constituents rarely see this, because it doesn't get reported. But time with a journalist usually reaps good rewards in terms of public profile.

The media is still very male-dominated. Female journalists make up just 25% of all journalists operating in Parliament,[4] and nearly all the editors of national newspapers are male. The media has an obsession with women's looks, what they wear, and how they behave. Even the wives of male MPs can get a slating for wearing something too expensive (e.g. Sarah Brown and her expensive Jimmy Choo heels and Samantha Cameron's M&S polka dot dress). Even being Prime Minister is no protection against sexist comments. Theresa May's kitten heels, cleavage, and jewelry were all fair game for comment in a way that David Cameron and other male PMs were never discussed.

No qualifications needed, but huge amounts of energy are
Anne continued: "Somebody once said it's a job that you need less qualifications for than any other job. You need no qualifications. But you do need phenomenal amounts of energy, because you can work very long days. You need to love what you're doing, don't you? I think if you love what you're doing, then you've got the energy to do it. It's a job like no other, it's extremely hard for the public to understand what it entails, and there is no job description".

On being a Whip
Anne: "We have a system in this country where the executive is drawn from Parliament, which isn't the same everywhere; I'm no constitutional expert. So if your party is in government, you're doing a second job as well, which is very busy, not for the faint-hearted. My job as a Whip was not simply about forcing people to vote in a certain way. The role of a government Whip's office is to get the business of government through the House and to make sure that the opposition has adequate time to oppose it. The feature of our democracy is that we think it's important for opposing views to be heard and that it's right and proper to have opposition parties. A Whip's job is a cross between a management lackey and a union steward; we bring the two sides of the argument together. Whips should manage up as well as down".

Nannying and counselling MPs

Anne: "There's quite a big pastoral role in the Whip's office. You've got maybe 300 MPs to manage and that's as good as it gets in terms of HR, with each Whip managing about 25 MPs. So in any organization with 300 employees, there's a mixture of people with all sorts of problems. And there's a range of personal and professional problems, so you're there to work through that".

Prioritising

Anneliese Dodds: "Prioritisation is important, because in my constituency, I need to have three full-time case-workers deal with the work coming into my office, when I know that talking to some of my colleagues in better-off rural areas, they have literally one person working half-time and that's enough. Being able to prioritise is challenging and it's the thing you need to quickly get good at.

"And there's always something urgent. Someone's about to be evicted because they can't pay the rent anymore, or someone's about to be deported because they've got problems with UK visas or whatever, they are really urgent. There are also people trying to contact you about a vote that's happening in Parliament the next week as well, so how can you balance those demands? That's a challenge, that's where having really good staff who know their stuff and are hard-working and reliable and caring is very important. And then prioritising work whilst you're in Parliament and also working out where you can have an influence and where you can't. There's no point spending a lot of time fighting a battle you can't win".

Collaborative working

Anneliese: "It's most rewarding working with others and getting to know what their issues are and seeing if you can collaborate. I particularly like bringing people together across different departmental teams. That's often when we can have the most impact. Also realising that sadly, no matter how hard you try, you're not going to please all of the people all of the time and that's just a fact of life".

Heidi Allen: "You have to be able to bring the right people around a table and be able to co-ordinate meetings. Every constituency is different, so your qualities may be dependent on whether you want to focus on being a constituency MP that's got busy casework, or whether you want to be Westminster focused and interested in certain types of legislation, then perhaps you need skills and knowledge in that area".

Passion, resilience, perseverance and a bit of a thick skin

Heidi Allen: "You need passion, resilience, a bit of a thick skin, but not too thick. A thick skin insofar as you can bounce back. Perseverance, you have to be confident in your views, you don't have to be an expert on everything. Some MPs try and pretend that they are, but certainly the most important quality is to listen, and to know when you don't know. I have my little black book, in which I'm gathering notes about 'this person was a GP and knows about medicine, this person was an engineer and knows about bus infrastructure' or whatever, but mental resilience, confidence, and the ability to listen are the most important things".

Jess Phillips: "There is no one way to be an MP, and all of the rhetoric around 'well, you should have had a real job first, we shouldn't have people who've done PPE at Oxford, it should be from down the pit', we need all of those people actually, in reality, though obviously it's skewed one way at the moment. I don't like that sort of politician bashing that everybody should have these certain things, because everybody has different skills and we need a whole range of skills".

Public speaking skills in Parliament are woeful
Jess: "One thing I have to say that I've noticed in here is that the level of public speaking is woeful. The ability to speak so that people outside of Parliament can hear you is a skill that is necessary, otherwise we're just talking to each other".

OK with people hating you
Jess: "You have to have a good nous to be a Member of Parliament, you have to be competent and pretty hard, because you have to be OK with people hating you, learning to be OK with that fact and going, 'well you can't please all the people'. And that's important. Trying to please everyone and do the right thing is a fool's errand. Also thinking too much that there's only one answer would make you a bad Member of Parliament".

Willingness to learn
Jess: "You've got to be willing to learn whilst you're here. Because what do I know about what it's like to grow up in a coastal town? What do I know about what it's like to live in a rural community? I don't know anything about it, and I might have the view 'oh, you shouldn't moan, you're getting loads of money from Europe', but that's ignorant and arrogant of me, from my position. So you've got to be able to learn to deal with other people and also have the ability to talk to people. Have some good chat lines, because you speak to a lot of people and a lot of different people. Being able to communicate with them all is important".

Physical fitness and health

Kate Green: "You need lots of energy and physical fitness, actually. You do need to be well to be an MP. It must be horrendously hard if you're not. You need to be tough, resilient, very resilient; you will be attacked a lot, sometimes quite personally. You do need to be articulate and good at presenting yourself, to lots of different people and lots of different situations".

Compromise and principled positions

Kate: "You need to be clear-minded to think through complexity and work out how you're going to trade off difficult compromises and arrive at a principled position. And you need to be principled. If you're not principled, you get lost, because so many of these decisions are difficult and it's hard to make them if you haven't got a clear basis of where you're coming from. You have to be prepared to compromise if you want to change anything".

Team players and lone wolves

Kate: "The team players are better than the lone wolves. That's not to say the lone wolves don't sometimes score spectacular successes. You also need to be good at details".

Proper job before coming into Parliament?

Kate: "Being an MP is a proper job and it's the hardest job I've done. I've worked in the private sector, the public sector, and the voluntary sector. I've worked at senior levels and junior levels, and this is, without question, the hardest job I've ever done. So I absolutely don't buy 'you should have had a proper job before you do this'. **This is the most proper job**. I can say with the benefit of nearly 30 years of professional life before I came to Parliament that this is the hardest job that I've ever done and people should know that".

"Is it helpful that I've had a broad career experience in those three sectors before coming to Parliament? Yes it is, because it means there are lots of things to draw on, things you recognize, patterns you understand. Is it essential? No. Some people are ready to do a brilliant job right at the beginning of their careers. And I do think Parliament needs to have a mix of ages and experiences, as it also needs a mix of gender, ethnicity, disability, and all the other things that make us different. I don't think you're a better or a worse MP just because you've done things before".

People person
Rosie Duffield: "You need to be a people person, because you're meeting people all of the time. You have to want to see change or make sure that we're talking about and dealing with things that are relevant to people, that are representative. Because there are only 650 of us and we represent 65 million people. So you have to have an eye on what's going on, you have to be aware of current issues and global issues, as well as nationally. The number one key thing is listening, because we are asked our opinion on things, every single day, e.g. 'What do you think you can do for young people?' 'Well, why don't you ask young people? Because you know, I'm not one anymore.'"

Open-mindedness and being tractable
Rosie: "So, listening is very important, also open-mindedness and being tractable, so not being entrenched in a view is very important. I've always been a bit like that, if you have a debate, be prepared to change your mind. To be swayed by someone who's got real knowledge on something, rather than just go in all guns blazing, 'I'm not changing my mind...', that's not progressive and that's not going to help move forward an issue or a campaign, you've got to be open-minded".

The "lived experience"
Sarah Wollaston: "You can be an MP with all sorts of qualities. As I look around the Chamber, there are all types of different people. There's no right way to be an MP, everybody does the job differently, there's no job description, and that's part of the strength of Parliament if it's going to be representative. You can't say this group of people are the wrong sort of people to be an MP, because then you don't have a representative Parliament which looks and sounds like the country it's seeking to represent.

"And I think we're really strengthened by the fact that now you can have a debate on almost any sort of subject and someone will pop up who's got some really relevant experience, and in health care, of course, that can be lived experience as a patient or as a carer. That can be just as valuable as a healthcare professional, having that combination of experience, so the thing that I find is that some people say 'I could never do the job because I've only ever looked after my parents as a carer.'"

Four criteria the selection panels look for
Caroline Spelman: "You have to make yourself accessible and you have to go the extra mile. And if you don't like people, it's not the job for you. It's very much about people. Some people are attracted into politics having seen the selection side of it, and we look for four criteria when we're doing selections, which are:

a) Obviously raw intellect: you've got to be reasonably bright to deal with it, you don't have to be a brain surgeon, you don't even have to have a degree, but you need to have a level of intellect which will allow you to grasp the issues that you're dealing with.

b) You've got to have good analytical skills and the ability to prioritise. If you can't prioritise, then you're going to be overwhelmed by it. Because you know you need to be able to quickly, with an interest up, pick up the files first thing in the morning. You have to know **this** is going to come first, I've got to deal with **this** right now, **that** can wait till this afternoon, and the **other thing** is going to take a long time to sort out. That ability to analyse, some people have it and some people don't.

c) Then, obviously, public speaking: a lot of people think that is the key criteria, but actually, the amount of times you speak in public, in the Chamber, it's not that often. People can get better at that in my experience, but then it's only one of four. And then here comes the most important thing, in my view, which is...

d) The ability to listen, because if you're not good at listening, you won't pick up the underlying problem. You'll misdiagnose what the problem is, whether it's in a surgery or whether it's listening to a debate. That ability to listen is very, very important".

References:

1.YouTube (2014) [online]. Available at: https://www.youtube.com/watch?v=XjJQBjWYDTs [accessed 26th May 2019].

2. The Independent (2018) [online]. Available at: https://www.independent.co.uk/news/uk/home-news/teenage-girls-self-harm-report-childrens-society-a8511686.html

[accessed 26th May 2019].

3. Plastic Surgery (2018) [online]. Available at:
https://www.plasticsurgery.org/documents/News/Statistics/2018/plastic-surgery-statistics-report-2018.pdf
[accessed 26th May 2019].

4. Parliament UK, Women in News and Current Affairs Broadcasting (2015) [online]. Available at:
https://publications.parliament.uk/pa/ld201415/ldselect/ldcomuni/91/91.pdf
[accessed 19th May 2019].

Chapter 5

How to Get Elected

The Parliament Project[1] was set up to provide advice and help for women who want to get into politics (whether as an MP or a local councillor). Its objectives were:
– get informed
– get inspired
– write your personal political plan

Pathway to Parliament

Join a political party -> help at the local level, understand the process of campaigning, go out canvassing, ask the locals, listen to key issues in the constituency.

National candidate approval process -> get on approved list.

Selection for local constituency -> get a list of all members, approach as many as possible for support.

Get selected as a parliamentary candidate for whichever party. Campaign to be elected (election campaigns last for six weeks, but many candidates may spend years building their local profile, gaining friends and influence).

You ask your national party to be selected as a PPC (Party Political Candidate). You don't say where, or which constituency. You then undergo an assessment process based on skills and competencies, which happens for all parties. You are not selected on who you know; you are interviewed with door-step role play. If you get onto the preferred candidate list, you then get to choose your constituency and can apply for any one. You don't have to live there, though it is recommended.

Once you've gone through the assessment process, you can be on the list for life, or until you ask to be taken off it (this depends on the party). Some parties just automatically roll you over from one election to the next, whilst others have time limits of ten years.

Independent MPs

Up until February 2019, Martin Bell[2], the famous BBC war reporter, had been the most recent independent MP, when he stood against Neil Hamilton, the sitting Conservative MP in Tatton, at the 1997 general election. Neil was embroiled in a sleaze allegation at the time, as were a lot of the Conservative Party, which helped to bring about the massive Labour lLandslide. In order to help Martin to win, the Labour and Liberal Democrat candidates stood down in Tatton, and he became known as "The Man in White", standing on an anti-sleaze platform. Neil Hamilton's 22,000+ majority was swept away when Martin won by over 11,000 votes, making him the first successful independent MP to win an election since 1951.

However, in February 2019, eight Labour and three Tory MPs (including Heidi Allen and Sarah Wollaston) resigned from their respective parties out of frustration with the Brexit process (for both Labour and the Conservatives) and the anti-Semitism issue within Labour. At the time of writing, they are independent MPs, and there has been some outrage from their various constituencies regarding whether they should stand down and trigger a by-election. This is an interesting debate, since the MPs are arguing a moral point, whereas their constituents are arguing that they stood on a false platform and no longer represent their interests. It is not in the remit of this book to discuss this fascinating debate further.

How much does it cost to become an MP? There is a government equalities office, which has a pot of money for disabled candidates, but for the vast majority, it seems to be very expensive. In her book *Why We Get the Wrong Politicians*, Isabel Hardman estimates £30k to £500k, depending on whether a candidate has to move house and/or give up their job and how often they have to stand before being successful. She only interviewed the successful candidates who had become MPs. There are many, many people out there who stood once, twice, or three times and gave up, having spent many thousands of pounds and achieving no success.

Justine Greening has held a variety of Cabinet posts, including Secretary of State for Education from 2016 to 2018 and Minister for International Development. She was elected an MP in 2005. Her first quote was "I'm too normal to be an MP". She was a Tory growing up in Rotherham, wasn't political at school or at university, and was put off by the types she saw in Parliament.

She had planned a career in business, but once she started, she realized she wasn't getting much satisfaction. Just having a steady job and money was not enough. She got into politics by volunteering to do leafleting for her local Tory Party and never made an active decision to be an MP: she was just happy to be on the ballot paper.

"Being an MP is a great way to stay fit! [She enjoys squash and sport.] I was asked to run for Council so I applied. There was a terrible photo on the leaflet, so I failed first time. Second time around, I got a better photo and leaflet and succeeded".

"You don't need to be an expert on party politics, because when you knock on the door, you get asked questions about local issues like potholes, etc. It was the late 1990s, and I just got voted in [to the council]".

"Just be yourself: your constituents just want someone who cares and is prepared to see things through". She enjoyed being a Councillor and got a real kick out of it. "I realised I enjoyed it far more than my business job. Someone suggested I go on a Parliamentary list, so I did, because I was thinking I wouldn't get selected and therefore wouldn't have to fight it. I ran for a Labour seat because I didn't want the pressure of a marginal. It cost me a few hundred quid".

"I didn't stop doing my job to run my campaign, I just combined things. People would think it weird if you turned up on the doorstep during the day and said you were a full-time candidate. Also, there aren't many people in their homes during the day, they expect you in the evenings. They like you to have a day job, it shows you're normal and live in the real world. Don't be put off by setbacks, that is normal. I would love to be anonymous, I don't like putting my name out there, and I have to be reminded to do press releases".

"Don't let money get in the way. I had no money, but the party will help. I had to ask them to pay my £600 deposit for the election, and they did. Don't let work get in the way either. Parliament is no longer an old gentleman's club. But we must be careful for women not to flat-line, like they have in Scandinavia, which is why I am here today". (at the Women of the World Festival.[3]).

"The parties ebb and flow about what they are. Typical week? Loads of constituency work (case studies) with locals asking about specific issues like Heathrow and plastic bags. I love my job because I can make a difference. There are no right or wrong answers in politics. Parliament is nowhere near good enough on BAME issues or disability, but it is much better now, it has changed massively in the last decade. The Speaker now tells people to behave. I don't regret a moment. The more disillusioned you are with politics, then the more reason to get into Parliament".

"With the 2017 Cabinet re-shuffle, what did I think when I was asked to leave the Department of Education and go to Health? At the time, I thought about what I would regret in politics; I had been happy in the Education Department and didn't feel the need to be a Cabinet Minister for a fourth time. I didn't come into politics for a career or to be someone, I just want to do things, not be something. I am happier being an MP".

"Do I get much trolling? Am I patronized? Yes, it has happened, but a big advantage in politics is to be underestimated. Get on with your actions and don't let them affect you, it's their problem, they can 'mansplain' all they like".

"How to break into a constituency where a safe MP just gets re-elected every five years? This is a problem. Some MPs will be in their seats for the next 30 years, and they're mostly men, which is why it's taking so long for women to increase their numbers in Parliament. To get to 50:50 will take 80 to 100 years at the current rate of change, therefore, we need swifter turnover".

What if you don't like the local party?
Justine: "Local party selection is like *Blind Date* at times, I would probably never have fitted into a solid Tory seat. If you don't like the local party, then don't stand, go somewhere else. I went round a few constituencies. Don't forget: you're doing

this because you enjoy it and want to make a difference.
Things to consider:
– your links to your constituency
– your residential situation
–- time (you can just be a paper candidate first time, but get experience of the selection process)
– money
– personal circumstances
– political experience
– opportunity

"I didn't put any of my own money in, but another MP said she had re-mortgaged her house. You will be expected to do fundraising. You have to pay £500 for the deposit, but if you put a call out for this, then generally a richer member will pay it for you".

Preet Gill, MP for Birmingham Edgbaston and first female British Sikh MP (quotes taken from her video interview on www.parliamentproject website[4])

Preet was born in Edgbaston in 1972. Her father drove the No. 11 bus and her mother was a seamstress. Preet credits her father and Lord King (the first Sikh Life Peer in the House of Lords) as her main inspiration for her ambition to enter politics. She has six younger siblings and was educated at Lordswood Girls School and Bourneville College, where she was elected student president.

Preet graduated from the University of East London with a first class degree in Sociology and Social Work. After graduating, she worked in a kibbutz in Israel and with street children in India. She was elected as a Councillor for Sandwell in 2012 and was selected to stand for Labour in Edgbaston in the 2017 election, winning with 55% of the votes. In July 2017, she was elected as a member of the Home Affairs Select Committee.

She is the Chair of the All Party Parliamentary Group (APPG) on Mentoring and Sikhs. In January 2018, she was appointed to the Shadow Cabinet as International Development Minister.

She says her biggest source of support was from the Local Government Association (LGA). They provided lots of leadership training, mentoring, and networking opportunities. The LGA also provides lots of support outside of the Council through networking and friendships.

She was one of 57 women on the Jo Cox Women in Leadership Programme. "This was a great course and I've stayed in touch with many of the women on it since". She thought she had until 2020 before an election campaign would transpire, but then Gisela Stuart, the existing MP, stood down unexpectedly, so Preet was catapulted into standing, and she does this sort of thing well. "It's important to shadow an MP and understand what the work entails. When you get elected, it's quite a shocking experience in terms of the things you have to do".

"With Labour, when you apply to become an MP, you have to complete a form, very succinct with a word count, so knowing your constituency is very helpful. I went for the interview in London and was told I had been successful that same evening (Thursday night), and I went out to launch my campaign on the Saturday morning. Note to audience: the 2017 election was exceptional, in that it was called in a hurry, so many candidates, including myself, were appointed based on a quick interview rather than a longer process of several role-plays over a whole day".

"I sat down with my Constituency Labour Party (CLP) and we put a strategic plan together. This was based on local data they have gathered over the years and the quality of this data is very important. This is why it's difficult for new parties to succeed overnight, because you need grassroot teams who are *au fait* with organizing campaigns and have good knowledge and data of the local constituency. My CLP team were depressed to start with, because Theresa May had called a snap election, when Labour were at an all-time low and the Tories were doing well in the polls".

Preet brought in a lot of her friends from her former employer Accenture, and they had many diverse skills. They devised their own strategy for the six-week campaign. They knew they couldn't knock on every door, so they had to devise a smart strategy. Lots of journalists told her the seat was going to become Tory. "You'll get a lot of that, so you need to have self-belief. I was determined I was going to win this seat". This was seen as a marginal seat. "You have to believe, because you have to inspire your team, mobilise volunteers to come out on your behalf and create an energy around your team. You need to have passion and interest and if you mobilise young people you can have great fun".

"Knowing where the gaps are is key, so you can mobilise people to fill the gaps. I brought in all my friends and family. You need finance and your CLP must be election-ready. Be creative, seek donors, a social media presence, and use videos. I wanted billboards, even though the CLP said they didn't have the money. You have to give and take, and know the battles you can win. Be clear on the lines in the sand.

"Each Ward has to have a plan. Have a key set of people, use your grid of roads, plan of activity, appoint owners of streets, use the skill sets of individuals, specific jobs for specific people. Those who have good sales skills, let them sell the key messages on the doorstep, and send each round with a good listener, so they can ask questions and take notes. Those who are project managers, let them manage the door- knocking campaign for the grid of streets".

"Time devoted? I was out every day for six weeks from 10am to 9pm, this is important to note. I wanted to give 100% effort, and being out with my troops every day was a part of this, it makes a huge difference. I have two daughters, who were aged 6 and 8 at the time of the campaign, and I didn't see them in the evening for six weeks. My husband looked after them during this time, so you do need to have good support".

Tips on how to widen your support
"Don't underestimate the level of support out there for you. You'll be amazed at the 'drag effect', the energy a campaign creates, friends of friends, multiplication factor. Have a clear plan. People need to know why you are focusing on specific Wards and what your key messages are for those Wards".

"The Tories had a very national plan, whilst I had a very local plan, I kept the messages local, the issues that really mattered to people on the doorstep;, being a local Councillor helps here. I knew the constituency and the issues. You also must listen, don't assume you know all the issues. It's important to ask what their issues are. Get volunteers to ask and make notes. Your messages and language are also key, leaflets must be clear, not waffly".

How to make the most impact in six weeks?
"The billboards were key! My face and name were plastered on billboards across the constituency. When I knocked on doors, people would say 'I know who you are and your policies, this is great'. Some people overestimate the power of social media, but it often becomes a limited forum of people

chattering endlessly to each other. There are great swathes of society that you will entirely miss if you just focus on this medium".

Barriers?
"There will be times when you get disheartened. Some days will be bad days when lots of people will say they won't be voting for you because of some recent issue that had impacted the party negatively…".

"You do have to have a view on most things, because people will ask you absolutely anything. You also have to know the Party view, and you also have to think out your own views and what is important to you. You will get asked hard and difficult questions and you must remember to tell constituents when you are giving your own private view and when it's the Party view".

"When you get disheartened, just look at the campaign strategy. We had it on the wall so everyone could see it. I got lots of invitations to hustings. I was clear that I was only going to do important ones. I was determined to speak to as many people as possible. I visited community groups and prominent people. Knowing which groups are active in which areas, reaching out to them, knowing how they align with you. Be at the school gates, school cuts were a massive issue at the time. We had a great campaign and I made history!"

"As the first female Sikh MP in the UK, I got phone calls of congratulations from around the world. Many were surprised there hadn't been one before".

Being an MP

"No-one shows you the ropes, and leadership is key. Only rely on yourself. You have to set up your own office, learn how to run a business and employ people. You need to decide what is important, and many things are trial and error. You will learn from your mistakes. Here we are in April, 11 months on from the election, and I'm still tweaking my office. Identify the skills gaps in yourself and your team. Don't feel too pressurized to cut corners. Constituents email you from day one, and you often can't reply for at least a week until the IT is set up".

"This job is a vocation, it can suck you in entirely to become 24/7. You really care about your team and your constituents. Care-wrap people. You will get lots of public speaking. Always be prepared! You can turn up to places and events as a guest, not expecting to speak, but then get put on the spot when someone hands you a microphone!"

Heidi Allen: "I was running a business with my husband in Hatfield and we were living in North London, and when I started applying for seats…. I mean, I thought at first that I'd have to do a no-hoper seat because that's traditionally how it's done, but Tory central office encouraged me to try for safe seats because they wanted more women in the Party, especially women from business, because we were better, weren't we?!"

"And so I was careful about where I chose, because my husband was going to run the business in Hatfield, we were living in North London, and I wanted a life. I don't have children, but even so, I still want a life, I want to see my husband and all those sorts of things. So wherever it was, he still had to be able to get to work, so we gave ourselves a radius, and then when you bolt on the fact that I wanted science and business and growth, because that's my background, it had to be something around Cambridge".

"South East Cambridgeshire came up first, and I'll let you Google to see what happened there". (There was a counting error of 23 votes, which would have given the seat to Heidi, but the error was discovered only after the counting officer had gone home.)

"And then South Cambridge came up and had I not been successful there, then I don't think I'd have applied for any more. Because it had to fit in with my life, although I didn't know anything about what happened in Westminster. I'm not a big one for establishment and rules, but I figured that it might not suit me very well, so I thought I'd better get somewhere that's busy and exciting, to keep my brain occupied, just in case I don't fit in in Parliament".

Getting through the recruitment process
Heidi: "You have to get through the recruitment process before you apply for seats. So, to get approved on the Parliamentary Candidates List (PCL), there are a few individual interviews where you meet the assessor, put in your CV, and fill in an application form. Then there's a one- day assessment process, a Parliamentary Assessment Board (PAB), which involves a series of interviews, role plays, making speeches, writing essays, and you're given five minutes to deliver a three-minute speech on a topic, which could be about anything".

"If you pass that, you are essentially approved, and then you get email notifications when seats become vacant, when an MP has retired, or resigned from a local association. And it's up to you which seat you apply for, and then you fill in a standard application form, which is clearly tailored to that area, and it's up to them whether they invite you for interview or not".

"The Parliamentary Candidates List is not a preferential list in terms of the top five getting preferential selection. In a regular election with enough notice, this won't happen. But if there's a last minute resignation, then central office might say 'you've got these three to choose from'. And likewise, in 2017, because it was such a short time window, I think they did some of that again. Normally, and that's not what happened to me, you just apply to the local association. The applications go via central office, so they can vet you and check you're on the list".

"Then all the applications get passed up to that particular constituency and they decide who they want to interview. That's important, because the local area has to choose whom they think will suit their locale, and somebody stuck in London doesn't know that".

"And you don't have to go and live in your constituency if you don't want. I mean, every MP is different, I know an awful lot who live in London and that's it, and they'll go and visit their constituency on a Friday, and a bit more during recess. It's one of the questions they'll ask you, and it's up to the candidates how they choose to answer that. I did, and I felt I should, and that's why I deliberately chose somewhere where my husband could get to work from. I didn't want to play that game where I was trying to pretend I lived in three places. So yes, we live there certainly, but I stay down in London during the week".

Gillian Martin, SNP
(quotes taken from her video interview on the parliament project website)[4]

Gillian is the SNP member of the Scottish Parliament for the Aberdeenshire East constituency. She grew up in Newburgh and was educated at Ellon Academy. Her parents have always been politically active. A graduate of the University of Glasgow, she worked as a lecturer in further education for 15 years, alongside running her own business in video production and training for the energy sector. She was also the manager of an emergency media response team for oil and gas companies for 10 years. She had to cease this business when she was elected to the Scottish Parliament.

She first became politically active during the Scottish Independence referendum. She helped found Women for Independence (WFI) and was on the executive committee as the member for the north-east region. She has continued to participate as an ordinary member of WFI since becoming an MSP. She joined the SNP on the 19th September 2014 on the morning after the Scottish Independence referendum.

"I got into politics via a circuitous route. I've been opinionated all my life, but despite coming from a political family, I was never involved in party politics and only got involved the day after the Scottish Independence Referendum".

"I joined the Women for Independence (WFI) group to get women's voices heard in Town Hall debates, because they were originally all male to start with. I set up a blog about my kids (to start with), but it gradually got more political. WFI contacted me and asked me to speak at one of their events, so I agreed. And if you do one of these events half decently, you get invited back. There weren't many women putting themselves forward. Most of the Independence referendum meetings were all old style, chaired by men with mostly all male speakers".

"So I got involved with WFI and found my voice and confidence. I had been a lecturer in Further Education, so I was used to speaking to people, but these were students, not the public. The public are harder to persuade than students. I got lots of feedback about my public speaking, so my confidence grew and I learnt lots. So, even though the Referendum went the wrong way, (in my humble opinion), I didn't want to give up and go home, and others told me not to. It takes someone else to say 'have you thought about standing?' And you say 'no' instantly, but then go away and think about it. I was asked to stand in the general election, so I did, but didn't get selected. I wasn't ready, still very naïve. But I was much more ready for the Scottish election and won the SNP seat for Aberdeenshire East".

"For those who have decided: you've already made the toughest decision. For those who haven't: if you've raised a family, worked in a business or the public sector, whatever you've done, just go for it! Don't rule out politics because you've not been there before. Everyone has a lot to give. The more you have done in life, the more experience you'll have to draw upon".

"Within 24 hours of being elected, write yourself a list of things you want to achieve and the areas you want to focus upon, because once you're in there, other things take over. You'll be on a daily and weekly treadmill which will take your eye off the things you want to achieve, so you need to keep going back to your list".

References:

1.The Parliament Project website (2019) [online]. Available at:
http://www.parliamentproject.co.uk/
[accessed 19th May 2019].

2. Wikipedia (2019) [online]. Available at:
https://en.wikipedia.org/wiki/Martin_Bell
[accessed 26th May 2019].

3. Women of the World Festival, Southbank, London, March 2018. Justine Greening's presentation on "How to Get into Parliament".

4. The Parliament Project website (2019) [online]. Available at:
http://www.parliamentproject.co.uk/webinars-1
[accessed 26th May 2019].

Other useful information:
Rules and Guidelines for Standing for UK Parliament:
www.parliament.uk/get-involved/elections/standing
Support within political parties:
 www.women2win.com (Conservatives)
www.lwn.org.uk (Labour women's network)
www.libdemwomen.org.uk (LibDem women's network)
https://greenpartywomen.org.uk (Greens)
www.womensequality.org.uk (Women's Equality Party)

All this information and further useful links available here:
http://www.parliamentproject.co.uk/parties-and-orgs/

Chapter 6

Running your own business

One thing that probably never occurs to prospective MPs is that, if elected, they will have to run their own business. MPs are given approximately £120,000 to employ staff, equip two offices, and manage two remote teams of people, which, depending on the constituency, are sometimes hundreds of miles apart. Fortunately, with modern communications, keeping in touch with each office is now much easier, but it must have been a nightmare in Poldark's time. In fact, it beggars belief how Westminster based MPs could have reasonably managed remote constituencies before the telephone was invented.

Because MPs have no job description, it is often taken as read that they will be all things to all people and have the necessary skills and training, but as interviews with most of the MPs for this book revealed, many felt they were lacking key skills when they arrived and also yearned for extra professional training and continuous professional development. When once Westminster MPs might have seemed to be ahead of the professional game because many were wealthy, came from the landed gentry, and would have been well educated and proficient in managing teams of people and budgets, much more adeptly than the average commoner, the opposite now seems to be the case, where your average office middle manager gets more CPD training in managing people, budgets, expenses, and leadership.

Management training programmes would prove useful to a lot of MPs (one of whom confessed she had never used a spreadsheet before entering Parliament) and certainly when your author worked at the Open University Business School, we talked about approaching Parliament with a portfolio of management training courses to see if they might be interested. Ten years on, a UK business school would do very well to train our political leaders better. The exposure of the expenses scandal in 2008 showed just how bad Parliament is at managing basic things that every small company up and down the country does without any problem. MPs telling the press how difficult it was to manage not just the practice, but also the principle of expenses shocked most people in the country.

Westminster seems to be failing on a lot of scores: expenses, maternity/parental rights and leave, the provision of a staff handbook and basic terms and conditions, sexual harassment, complaints and appeals, anti-Semitism/racial and sexual discrimination, and the whole process of "Whipping", which would be classified as employee abuse in any other business and thrown out. Heckling, cheering, shouting, and booing: all those Chamber behaviours that we witness on TV would also not be tolerated in a modern office environment. Also, the abilities to manage staff, negotiate professionally, take on board other views, and compromise are skills massively lacking amongst all the leading parties, which has been exposed, to national disgust and shame, during the Brexit debacle.

Professor Sarah Childs spent two years living in Parliament researching and observing what goes on. In her excellent Good Parliament Guide (discussed in greater detail in Chapter 11), she made 43 recommendations for improving gender equality. It is worth looking at those suggestions from another perspective, which highlighted the archaic processes still going on. Just in terms of time efficiency, it is amazing that Westminster has still not introduced electronic voting. Many MPs justify this on the grounds that you can get to buttonhole a specific Minister that you've been trying to pin down for ages and therefore going into the Chamber in person can save five separate meetings. But does this really happen? Whilst dutifully filing through the "ayes" or the "nos", does an individual MP really get more than a fleeting minute to have an off-the-record chat with whichever Minister? And being un-minuted or recorded, is this chat worth the paper it isn't written on? And can you really manage to see five of them?

What is it that an MP actually does?
The Good Parliament Guide recommended that an MP's job description be written down – this was back in 2016, though it still hasn't been done – but the five key components of being an MP were outlined as follows:

1. Constituency work
2. Speaking in the Chamber, working on committees, APPGs, writing/unpicking legislation, PR
3. Working for your Party (generically)
4. Pursuing your own interests/passions (and furthering them via Private Bills etc.)
5. Being an employer/running two offices/managing a business

In addition, an MP can be promoted to Minister, Whip, or sit on any number of Committees (of which there are 123 at the time of writing).

Parliament[1]

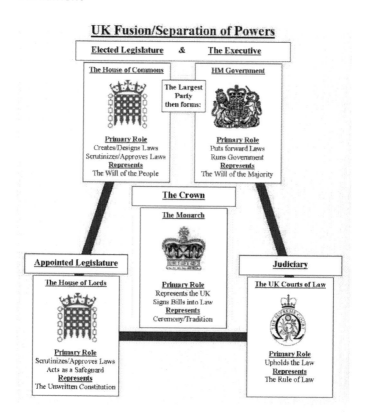

UK Fusion/Separation of Powers

Elected Legislature & The Executive

The House of Commons

Primary Role
Creates/Designs Laws
Scrutinizes/Approves Laws
Represents
The Will of the People

The Largest Party then forms:

HM Government

Primary Role
Puts forward Laws
Runs Government
Represents
The Will of the Majority

The Crown

The Monarch

Primary Role
Represents the UK
Signs Bills into Law
Represents
Ceremony/Tradition

Appointed Legislature

The House of Lords

Primary Role
Scrutinizes/Approves Laws
Acts as a Safeguard
Represents
The Unwritten Constitution

Judiciary

The UK Courts of Law

Primary Role
Upholds the Law
Represents
The Rule of Law

Training and getting started

Heidi Allen made four videos[2] available on YouTube about her first four weeks in Parliament in 2015 and how it took three weeks just to get her office up and running. This waste of time is surprising in the 21st century when MPs have an important job and time can be critical for some constituents facing eviction, prison, or even death at the hands of a violent partner. Being unable to contact an MP because their office is not up and running is not acceptable in the 21st century, and

Parliament should set itself some turn-around targets, like everyone else in the UK.

In organisations of a similar size, there would be an IT manager/director ensuring a smooth transition from one MP to another. Computers, mobile phones, passwords, and office furniture would be in place before the MP arrived. That Heidi Allen had to wait three weeks for a carpet to be put in when the election date had been known for months means that no-one is managing the process: it is left down to individual MPs. These MPs arrive in a flush of elation and exhaustion from a tough election campaign and have a hundred issues on their plates from day one. Constituents are emailing them from the minute their election victory is announced, but it may be two to three weeks later before they get access to that email and start tackling the backlog.

Rosie Duffield:
"You don't get any training when you enter Parliament. The Labour Party do their best and tell you how to get an office and do a little bit of training, but mostly everyone is just too busy. You are kind of left to your own devices. When we got here, I was given a buddy who works for Parliament, not a Labour buddy, which was fabulous".

"I had a great woman who worked for digital services who told me **so** much, like 'this is where you go for your security, this is where the loo is, etc.'. I couldn't really have found my way round without her, she was wonderful. But in terms of learning really what happens, it's very difficult, you're on your own. I didn't realize how much, and from day one, there's a phone ringing somewhere. Even before you get an office, you're given a phone number and email account, so I was elected on the 9th June and I didn't get here until about the 14th, because that's what we do. And already I'd got hundreds and hundreds of emails and no computer.

"So the public are going 'why hasn't she answered her email?', because I've got no computer and no idea I've got an email address. So that's really a pretty crap way of doing things, actually! And from that minute, we have to set up an office. So, a lot of Labour MPs will have been moved into a retired seat or have inherited the office of their predecessor. We (Labour) didn't have an office in Canterbury and have never had one.

"So, we had to think, well, how do we get an office? What do we do? Things take weeks and weeks. How do I get staff? What's my budget? How do I even advertise? You know, all of that was brand new to me. There was a bit of help, but when it came to asking IPSA (the Independent Parliamentary Standards Authority) 'what do I do about buying furniture or renting a place?', their answer seemed to be 'well, lots of MPs just do that and then they can claim back'. And I said 'but I've got no money!', and they were absolutely taken aback, they didn't seem to know what to do about that. Because I think that most people who come in are married or have had a successful or well-paid career or have been doing something similar.

"I was a teaching assistant, I was a single mum. I had literally no money. You don't get paid for anything when you're campaigning, so I'd been borrowing money off people and got myself into debt. And I said 'but I can't afford the rent for an office or even a chair! What do I do?' So, eventually we (the Labour Party locally) had to work all of that out between us. That was really difficult. You had to set up a business account, as a small business, put your own money in, and then get reimbursed. I didn't have the money to open a business account. What makes me annoyed about that is we say we're inclusive and we want ordinary people to be in Parliament, but that process is very prohibitive. Had I known that, I wouldn't have stood, because I couldn't have afforded to. But I didn't know that and I didn't know I'd win, so that was academic, I guess".

Rosie actually had to take out a personal loan to fund the acquisition and setting up of her office in Canterbury. Labour HQ wouldn't lend her any money, and it speaks volumes for how much the Labour Party is unused to non-wealthy MPs that they had no loans process to help her out. Wouldn't you imagine that the Central Labour Party would have a load of funds they could dip into?

Rosie: "Yes, but this is all Parliamentary money, which is different. I don't think the Parties are allowed to fund that sort of thing. I've also found out that my predecessor, his local party (Conservative) paid for his staff and his premises, which was operated from his house, and he employed his wife! So, I've used up all of the office budget that you're allowed, where he spent none. I've spent all of that because I want a full staff and an office and somewhere where people can go, because we need to deal with all the case work. I know I've already done a lot more work than he did, case wise. So I'm glad I've done that. People don't really know how all of this works".

"There's no formal induction process, but the Labour Party are brilliant, and I know I could have asked anyone, but all the newcomers, we were sharing information on a WhatsApp group, asking 'What do we do? What's the budget? What do we do about tax?' and just kind of learning that way. It is a very complicated expenses system and it's incredibly easy to get caught out. You know, declaring things, not declaring things.

It's a minefield. I had never worked in business or run my own business, so I hadn't a clue how that side of things worked".
"So, that was sorting out my constituency in Canterbury, whilst in Westminster, the Labour Party assigns offices to its own MPs. So the Whips did that and I was really happy to share with a colleague (Anneliese Dodds), so we got an office reasonably soon, about two weeks in. Other people were waiting weeks and weeks, depending on how quickly you got in there. It was a big scrabble for everyone to sort their offices out. But yes, I was OK, I share with my colleague Anneliese, and it's a really nice place".

Hiring staff and managing budgets
Rosie: "I had no training on budget management, but my office manager is brilliant and she's managing that side of things. There's a budget for your staff and you can employ up to five. I've gone to the maximum. One of my case-workers, for example, is almost exclusively focusing on asylum and immigration cases, because of where we are. You don't really know how things are going to pan out. We've got another who is almost completely focused on housing, because that's another huge issue where I am. And then we've got a couple of people who can tackle different things, but yes, you don't really know until you start getting those cases in, what your work load is going to be comprised of".

Parliamentary HR department
Rosie: "There is a Parliamentary HR department, yes. And I had a query with one of my staff at the beginning and they were very helpful with that. So, you can go to them as a sort of advisory or recruitment service. But they aren't in charge of line managing or resolving HR issues or complaints. You are basically managing your own staff. You are self- employed and

running your own mini-business, so the buck stops with the MP".

Training and support for MPs?
Should you have basic business skills such as finance, marketing, management before you become an MP?

Chi Onwurah: "Well, it's important that anyone should be able to become an MP. I don't think there should be requirements on having a certain background, or certain experiences. I find my MBA (from Manchester Business School) incredibly helpful, in what, in effect, is managing a small business. It's helpful in terms of people management and in terms of organization, and what I've found is that there's very little formalized personal development for MPs or their staff, so I've made it a requirement that all my staff should do at least one week's personal development training per year.

"But there is very little that is formalized like that and almost none for MPs. I think the only training we can claim for is media training and strangely, language training. So I do think there should be more training and support for MPs".

"The induction training I had here lasted about half a day and was all about the different types of questions you could ask. There was nothing about how to effectively run two offices, here and in my constituency. So I do think management and particularly people management training would help. You've seen all the things about bullying? I think some good people management training would help immensely".

Jacquie Smith was only the third woman to hold one of the Great Offices of State, after Margaret Thatcher (Prime Minister) and Margaret Beckett (Foreign Secretary). In an

125

interview with *Total Politics* magazine regarding her time as Home Secretary, Smith described how she felt under-qualified for her Ministerial roles, adding: "When I became Home Secretary, I'd never run a major organization. I hope I did a good job. But if I did, it was more by luck than by any kind of development of skills. I think we should have been better trained, there should have been more induction".

Time taken to get installed in your new office
Heidi Allen: "So every General Election, there's a bit of a flurry, because strictly speaking, when an election is called, you're supposed to move out of your office and wait and see if you are re-elected. But in reality, for those who have safe seats, you kind of don't. But I think what happened in the 2015 election, there was a really big shift in seats, so it was a bit chaotic with loads of people moving out, loads of people moving in. And the facilities team just need a bit of time to work their way through that. Sometimes offices are shared, so one could be moving out without the other, so it can be like a big jigsaw, so yes, it can take quite a bit of time.

"And the previous incumbent took the carpet as well. I think it must just have been a room they had chosen to re-furbish. I think that's what added an additional delay. Perhaps the previous MP had been in there for decades, and they decided it needed a complete refresh".

"You can spend part of your budget on IT and there's a limit to that budget. And that's for all the equipment in your office here and back at your constituency, and you can choose how to spend that. Personally, I have chosen to use my own laptop, because I just think it's taxpayers' money, it's 10.30pm at night here, I want to Google and arrange a Sainsbury's shop for back home, so I want to do that on my own computer, not a

Parliamentary machine. Perhaps I'm being a little bit over-sensitive and the team all have Parliamentary machines, but I like to use my own laptop".

"When we went into Parliament, we had a little bit of training. As I remember, I was told our 2015 intake had a better induction than previous. I can only speak for the Tory Party obviously, but I was told that in 2010, even more Tories came in that year and so it was a bit more chaotic still than we had. There is a little bit of 'oh these are the key people to speak to for this…'. But the way the place operates, the Parliamentary procedures, the amendments, how you do an amendment, how a Bill works, there' is none of that, you sort of have to find that out for yourselves".

"There is an HR department, but that's more related to helping you employ staff and things like that. Your Whip, I suppose, is the go-to person, but as I mentioned earlier, Whips can be difficult".

CPD and basic employment rights
"I have one member of staff down here, two full-timers and a two-thirds full-timer in the constituency. By law, we don't have the right to four weeks holiday or sick pay. It's a funny thing, you're not self-employed, but you don't have a contract either, there's nothing. No staff handbook, terms and conditions of employment, nothing like that, no holidays, no contractual pay, no, nothing at all".

Kate: "There are briefings and occasional training events. There's one being offered at the moment on data protection. Most MPs go to hardly any of those, myself included, you learn on the job mostly".

Inspiring female role models?
Kate Green: "I think like every other woman in the Labour Party, Harriet (Harman) has been a huge inspiration to all of us. But I haven't ever really had a woman that mentored or that helped with my own personal development, no. I've never had the need, to be honest. I found it more useful to know that there was a big group of women collectively, fighting for a better deal for women.

"For me, I don't think it's been necessary to have a mentor in Parliament. I don't want that one-to-one relationship. But a lot of other women I know have benefitted from this sort of relationship, or at least say they have. I don't want to have a mentor, nor to be one. I tried it a little while being one for the Fabian Women's network, and I just said 'this is not a role I fulfil well'. When I was first elected, I was helpfully supported by Barbara Kealey, but that was just to tell me the facts. I could go to Barbara and ask her 'what's this on the order paper, I don't understand what we're doing here'. It wasn't about personal development or how to present myself in Parliament, or how to position myself. I didn't feel a need for that".

Mentors
Sarah Wollaston: "I don't have a mentor and when I arrived, I wished I did. But of course, what you find is that people who are already well connected have the mentoring, whereas people who arrive from outside are left on their own to find out how the job works. For new MPs, when I arrived in 2010, it was pretty much non-existent. It was like 'here's a laptop, here's a desk to hot desk with, get on with it!' There wasn't any training, and I regret that, because had I known then what I know now, I could have influenced things differently".

"Because what you do need to know is how you can influence and make a difference. It's not just about standing up and making a speech in the Commons. On the big scale of things, that makes less impact than actually using other methods that you have, to try and influence things. So I think having a mentor for a new MP who doesn't know things is a very good thing".

Rosie: "I don't have a mentor, though all the Labour women have always said 'just ask', you know, and I have. We have that Labour all-women WhatsApp group, where one of us will go 'help, I don't know how this works' or 'can you do this any other way?' and we're all there to help each other".

Would it be useful for everyone to have a formal mentor?
Rosie: "It's a great idea, but I'm not sure how it would work in terms of there just probably isn't the time, to be honest. Just not sure anyone could dedicate that time to doing it. It's a good idea, I mean you have a Whip, and I was so lucky, when I got here, my Whip was always saying 'are you OK?' 'do you want a coffee?' 'come into my office'. And I knew whatever questions I would have, she could answer. And she was just brilliant and she's now the Whip for my team, so that's a really positive thing".

Heidi: "I was lucky, I had a good friend, David Burrowes, who took me under his wing and taught me all the clever things you can do with amendments, things I shouldn't have known from my short tenure here, but he taught me how to get through the nitty-gritty of legislation and change things or attempt to. The process of how you table questions, how you put in to speak, who the ministers are, who the departments are, who the diary secretaries are, you get told none of that, you have to find that out for yourself. Sadly, David lost his seat in the 2017 election, so now I don't have a formal mentor. I've got maybe half a dozen more senior MPs to bounce ideas off, who I can talk to".

References:

1. Parliament diagram reproduced by kind permission from the House of Commons library.

2. YouTube (2015) [online]. Available at: https://www.youtube.com/results?search_query=heidi+allen+MP+weeks+1
[accessed 3rd Nov 201

Chapter 7

"I absolutely love it" – Jess Phillips

"It's the best job in the world" – Anne Milton

"I love being an MP and it is a great privilege to spend your time pursuing what you believe in" – Jo Swinson

The highs and lows of being an MP

Despite the workload, every MP interviewed for this book said they loved their job. "No two days are the same", "it's a 24/7 vocation", and "the only skill you need is passion and to care, you learn everything else on the job". "It's one of the few jobs in the country where you don't need any qualifications, there is no job specification and no appraisals!"

Jess Phillips is renowned for repeatedly sticking her head above the parapet, reading out the names of the 120 or so women who lose their lives at the hands of their violent partners in Parliament every year on International Women's Day. Jess has come out with such gems as "every man sitting the house is now here because at some point, his mother had a period[1]" and "I would knife Jeremy Corbyn in the front, not the back[2]".

Jess has a deep voice and a fantastic sense of humour. Her recent book *Everywoman: One Woman's Truth About Speaking the Truth*[3] should be mandatory reading on the national curriculum, because it teaches girls (and boys), in a funny and readable format, exactly what is wrong with our gendered society of today. She's great on Twitter, very courageous, and doesn't back off from the huge numbers of trolls who daily try to grind her down with their abuse, hiding behind their anonymity whilst she has to face them in the full glare of being a public MP.

"I absolutely love it, and it's terribly clichéd to say it's a massive privilege to have a voice and to fight on behalf of people. The best bit of my job is being with my constituents in Birmingham, knocking on doors and meeting lots of different sorts of people. And I like the actual job of standing up and speaking, or writing things or pushing policies. And I really, really like the social work element of it as well, so you get to do both".

"The thing that makes me want to do cartwheels is when you win something, and you get those weekly. Those proud moments when you win something for a constituent, like you win a tribunal, you'll win getting somebody a new house, and those are brilliant moments. And there's a real team effort to it that makes you feel really, really proud. I'd say in Parliamentary terms, my proudest achievement is just actually getting every policymaker who I ever come across to remember that (a) women exist and that (b) domestic violence, well, violence against women and girls, needs to be taken into consideration in how they think about the economy. Or in how they think about housing strategy, it's just that you're sort of like a reminder".

"But the thing that I feel proudest of at the moment is every year, I stand up and do that reminding by reading out the names of women who would be completely forgotten, who have been murdered by their partners, to continue to make the point. And I feel very, very proud when their families get in touch with me and say, 'you know, without you, she would just have been another number on a sheet. She was just another statistic that politicians spout and you made her real, and you remembered her, and that's really nice'".

Pointing to the wall of cards: "I get a lot of thank you cards. And the ones that we get here are not for things that we do in the constituency. My constituency office is, literally, the walls are plastered with thank you cards, and that's for thanks for sorting out my bins or thanks for getting my kid into school. The ones here are from people that are saying thank you for speaking, thank you for your voice. Thank you for representing us, when you said something about this".

"None of this is personal to the people that you've helped, this is about the things that you've said that have meant something to somebody. And that's really nice to be surrounded by.... I get fan mail every single day, so that is nice. I get much more fan mail than I get hate mail. But the newspapers like to write about the hate mail. I get loads of thank you cards, stuff from kids in schools, it's brilliant".

It's important that readers are aware of the last point, since the media focuses so much on trolling and hate mail, which every single MP interviewed for this book said was just a very small part of their job, but was being over-emphasized by the misogynistic media, often almost revelling in the idea of women being silenced.

More female MPs = more women's issues discussed
They say if you're not at the table, you will be the dinner. It's taken women an awfully long time to realize this. Put a lot of men in a room together and they will either entirely ignore women's issues, with the law of unplanned consequences kicking in, such as zero childcare, maternity leave, period

poverty, abortion regulation, lack of pension provision, unequal pay, domestic violence, and many other issues.

Or even worse, as happens in many Middle Eastern and African countries, the men will enact discriminatory legislation to better control their women. In the UK, we should be grateful we were mostly ignored for centuries, otherwise we might not even be allowed to drive today.

Since the June 2017 election, women now make up 32% of all MPs in the House of Commons, which is an all-time high and places the UK Parliament 38th out of 188 countries in the world[4]. Rwanda, Cuba, and Bolivia occupy the first three places and are the only countries where women make up more than 50% of the MPs in their Parliament. It seems surprising that these countries have better gender equality than the Scandinavians: perhaps we can conclude that women only get equality in a post-conflict situation, when a lot of the men are dead.

The increased numbers of female MPs in Westminster are finally enabling discussions about subjects that until recently were total taboo. Periods, sanitary wear, abortions, consent, and rape have been a big deal to women over the centuries, but have rarely had any mention in the male corridors of power. It is interesting that only the aspects of women's lives which have a monetary value get much attention in the press, such as equal pay, pension poverty, and more recently, the financial cost of domestic violence (male politicians weren't much interested in the deaths).

Abortion rights
Heidi Allen broke down in tears when talking about her own termination in the debate about de-criminalising abortion in

Northern Ireland[5]. This personal experience is one that cannot be told by men, and listening to it brings an emotive and pragmatic perspective that was lacking in the original 1967 debates when David Steel brought forward his private member's bill to legalise abortion in Great Britain. This excluded Northern Ireland, where the religious bigots are still demanding the right to control women's bodies to the present time.

Tampon tax

Stella Creasy forcing Sir Bill Cash to say the word "tampon" was another breakthrough[6]. These are discussions that should have been had years ago, but thank goodness, they are finally having their day, and what a difference they make. The injustice of the "tampon tax"[7] had to be spelt out to male politicians, because it simply hadn't occurred to them. The idea that tampons and other sanitary products could be classified as "luxury" items and hence subject to VAT beggars belief. How did the average male MP think women were coping if they went without these "luxury" items? Locking themselves up for five days every month?

The Tory government blamed the EU, saying that their rules stopped them from scrapping the tax, but in March 2016, it accepted a proposal by a Labour MP to end it once and for all. It has been reduced from 10% to 5%, and with Brexit looming, this might finally be sorted, but as ever, fishing rights and the Irish backstop are higher up the agenda than something which affects one half of the population every month for the majority of their working lives. Colleen Fletcher asked the Secretary of State what steps have been taken to end period poverty, another subject that a majority male Parliament has never discussed since the dawn of time[8].

The home use of the abortion pill was a campaign fought and won in 2018, when a young woman (Claudia) spoke out about her use of it and the risk of miscarrying when having to travel home from the clinic on public transport. Her case was taken up by the Women's Equality Party and finally the Health Minister, Matt Hancock, agreed that the pill could be taken by women in the comfort of their homes rather than, as demanded by the outdated law in place, in a clinic or doctor's surgery[9].

The law had originally been written in 1967, when 100% of abortions were clinical procedures, but the development of the abortion pill, Mifepristone, which was approved for use in 1991 up to the ninth week of gestation, meant this was a law needing to be re-written. Only a focus from women enabled this situation to be corrected. This is another example where a majority male Parliament had failed to address this issue for 27 years, with many women struggling to get home from the clinic before massive bleeding began.

Parliament has still not addressed the inequity of women from Northern Ireland not being able to get an abortion on the NHS, but it seems certain that the determination of women like Jess Phillips, Stella Creasy, and Heidi Allen will soon prevail. They are on the right side of history, unlike the DUP. It is a huge shame on our society that hundreds of young women have to fly from Northern Ireland at their own expense each year to get abortions in England on the NHS. They should submit their expenses to the DUP and the Church.

Gender pay gap reporting
Justine Greening has been the Tory MP for Putney since 2005. The daughter of steelworkers in Rotherham, she was educated in a state comprehensive. She is your "girl next door", down to

earth, and it's heartening to see that such a normal person has been a Cabinet Minister three times. You feel empathy with her immediately: she is attractive in a natural way, nothing is quite perfect about her, and you can empathise with the effort she has made to look smart that morning. When I bumped into her on the stairs at the Women of the World Festival in the Southbank, she apologized, even though it was my fault.

As Minister for Women and Equalities, her key achievement was gender pay gap reporting[10]. "I knew when that regulation went through Parliament (laughs) that we were starting off something that would steadily have wave upon wave of impact, and so it proved. Also, we set ourselves a real ambition. Our team debated what percentage of reporting we should expect, and I said 100%, like everyone should do it. This isn't like 'if we get 90% what a great job'; I said '100%, that's what you're going for', a no-excuses approach to it".

Not always "I" but "we" – teamwork
Kate Green has been the Labour MP for Stretford and Urmston since 2010 and was selected through an All-Women's Shortlist. Her short cropped hair and no-nonsense manner give you confidence that she doesn't suffer fools lightly and that she'll make things happen for you. "It's a privilege to be an MP, because so few people get the chance to do this. It's great to be trusted by constituents to represent them and speak for them in the place where laws are made and scrutinized. And you make wonderful relationships with your constituents and your constituency, which I really enjoy".

When asked what achievement she is most proud of, Kate had a simple answer: "I don't really have one. There's none of this 'well I did that and I made the difference', because the things that I'm proudest of achieving are things we've done as a team. I'm proud of being the Shadow Minister when we put the Same Sex Marriage Act through Parliament. We were the opposition and the government would claim credit for that, rightly, as well. I'm also proud of the work I did, again cross-party, on Mesothelioma, a fatal lung cancer, asbestos-related, which is quite common in my constituency".

"We fought hard to improve the compensation scheme for sufferers. We didn't achieve all they deserved, but I was proud of getting to know them and making their case here in Parliament, and I'm really proud of being an MP. The night that I was first elected, you're grinding through the campaign and you're never quite sure whether you will win, and that moment when the result was announced, there was a surge of energy that went through me and I thought 'my god, I've done it'. Because, you know, I wasn't young, and it wasn't the first time I'd tried, so it was a huge thrill".

Gender stereotyping in engineering

Chi Onwurah has been the Labour MP for Newcastle Central since 2010 and is their first-ever black female MP. She is a striking individual: tall, with wild hair that refuses to be tamed by the conventions of the Commons. Unlike a lot of other black women, who spend disproportionate amounts of time and effort making their hair look more British, Chi shows hers with pride. "It's the best job in the world, but also the hardest job I've had, so I do enjoy my work hugely. There's nothing better than standing and speaking on behalf of the people you grew up with and that you want to represent. It can be challenging and frustrating at times, but what is important is the sense that you're making a difference".

Chi has campaigned passionately against gender stereotyping. She supported the "Let Toys be Toys" campaign and stated:

"Before entering Parliament, I spent 20 years as a professional engineer, working across three continents. Regardless of where I was, or the size of the company, it was always a predominantly male, or indeed all-male environment. But it's only when I am walking into a toy-shop that I feel I am really experiencing gender segregation".

The proportion of female students studying engineering degree courses has fallen from 12% to 8% in the last 40 years,[11] and at 10%, the UK has the lowest percentage of professional women engineers in Europe, with Latvia, Bulgaria, and Cyprus at 30%. Even India, a country not renowned for its gender equality, has over 30% female engineers. Chi said: "Toys are so important and formative, and this is about the jobs of the future and what happens in 10 to 15 years' time". There is a nationwide shortage of engineers, and if we enabled women to fulfil their potential and make up the shortfall, this could add as much as £28 trillion to national GDP by 2025. That's more than the cost of Brexit, but does this fact occupy any time on mainstream TV?

Female engineers are almost guaranteed well-paid, full-time jobs in engineering, and a survey of existing female engineers shows that 84% are happy or extremely happy with their job choice. Similar amounts of boys and girls take STEM GCSEs, so what is happening at A-level that only 20% of girls take A-level physics and this hasn't changed in 25 years? We need a sea change in the approach of mostly white, male, pale, and stale physics teachers towards their subject and its appeal to young women.

They could start with applying some of the standard classroom physics problems to issues that might interest the female half of the audience rather than the usual tedious car acceleration and refraction of light through prism questions. If they made questions about light refraction through sexy spectacles, the strength of nylon tights, and the reaction of hair towards heat, then girls might start to get interested. When I mentioned this to some friends, there was huge hilarity, which shows just how gendered our society is. The lack of physics graduates going on to do anything with their subject afterwards says there is also a problem at the university level, but no-one is demanding change. Chi again: "We can't go on with a segregated society and not fulfilling the potential engineering talent of 50% of the population".

Dedication to the job and shared parental leave
Jo Swinson's proudest moment as an MP was when she was a Minister and introduced Shared Parental Leave. It's a policy she was passionate about, and strategically, she thinks it is important for gender equality. "We're not going to reach a more gender-equal world when there's such inequality in the way caring responsibilities are divided in the home. Shared parental leave is one of the ways, it's a step in the right direction to normalising gender equality. Men and women jointly sharing the caring responsibilities is equally important for young children and old people alike".

She has fought passionately for women's rights over the years. In her book *"Equal Power and How You Can Make It Happen"[12]*, she states that the government has limitations when addressing gender equality and mainly suggests ideas for people to change their personal lives or workplaces. She was originally against positive discrimination and gender quotas, suggesting that persuasion and a change of culture should be enough. But she admits that in 2016, she changed her mind because of the appallingly slow rate of change. It is estimated that at the current rate of change, it will take another 50 or 60 years to reach equal representation in Parliament. (It's taken 100 years for us to get to 32%.) The World Economic Forum[13] has estimated it will take 217 years for the pay gap to close. PWC have estimated that economic parity for women could add £188bn to the UK GDP each year. This is another fact that should be getting more attention than Brexit. Sadly, this estimate has gone up since 2016, when it was "only" 170 years to reach pay parity.

Constituency vs. Westminster

Justine Greening: "I love being an MP in my local community, in a sense it's always started and finished there, but I also like the fact that in Westminster, you have a bigger impact on the country, and sometimes you can be the person who says something that articulates what a lot of people think, even when it's not that fashionable".

Jess Phillips: "There are things I don't like about being an MP. I don't like coming to London every week any more, and I cheer at the moment that I get to go home. I feel physically better and healthier and happier when I'm at home, which is understandable. That's where my children live, that's where my husband lives, that's where my house is. When I first came, it was really exciting to live both in London and in Birmingham and tick off both options, but that has worn off, and I just think I would be more productive if I was just in one place. But that's life and that's not going to change".

"I could move here, I suppose, and that's what lots of people do, they move to London. But I would sooner move to the moon than move to London, (a) because it's really expensive and (b) because none of my family or friends live here. And I don't like lots of elements about it. I don't like what politics is becoming, which is basically just an angry fight, rather than a collective call for action, and so I don't like that".

Intellectual challenge and big moments in politics?
Kate Green: "I particularly like scrutinizing legislation, I really enjoy the intellectual challenge around that. It's not a superficial job; that kind of work is detailed and intricate, and it's exciting to be where some of the big issues are going on at the time they're happening. So, the debates going on right now about Russian aggression or the Syria votes, they are major turning moments in politics and public life and it's exciting to be present and part of them".

You suspect that Kate is one of those dedicated MPs to whom Isabel Hardman refers in her book *Why We Get the Wrong Politicians.*[14]". Kate does lots of work in committees, because by her own admission she enjoys she enjoys scrutinizing legislation. To date, she has been a member of twelve 12 Public Bill Committees, a member of six Select Committees (and currently chairings two of them), and the chair of two APPGs. As Isabel Hardman states in her book, there isn't much public reward for doing this work, other than in heaven and for one's own conscience. Taking coffee with a journalist and getting some media sound bites stands you in better stead.

Second career, the perfect job for returning mothers?
Anne Milton had four children who were aged 9, 12, 18, and 21 when she was first elected an MP, and she was able to successfully bring them up whilst a serving MP and with a partner who gave up some of his working week to help support her. "For me, this is a second career, and that probably makes a difference, I was nearly 50 when I got elected. And how you view it depends on when you do it in

your career. It's varied, flexible, it fits in quite well with family life".

"If you take equivalent jobs at the same salary, it fits in more easily with family life than many other jobs, because you've got a lot of autonomy. If you were earning £75k a year, working for a local authority, you wouldn't have as much flexibility as you do as an MP".

"Parliament sits four days a week and 13 Fridays a year, but only essentially in school term times. You're not required to be here for votes every one of those days. On a Friday, unless you're a Minister, you don't have to be there, and on a Thursday, you rarely have to be here for votes. On a Monday, you don't have to be here before 3.30pm in the afternoon. So that's a lot of flexibility in your working week. The life you lead depends a bit on where your constituency is, the job is what you make of it. Although you don't have to be there for votes, there are Select Committees, Bill Committees, and debates you may well want to, or need to, attend. Nine out of ten people that take time off for caring responsibilities are women, and it's a job with a lot of flexibility".

A vocation, not a job
Anne: "The compulsory hours are limited, and don't believe anybody who tells you differently. They are long hours, but it's not a job, it's a way of life. It's like being the local vicar. You don't have a working week as such. You might be doing things on Saturdays and Sundays, in the evenings, in the holidays. You certainly work in the holidays, but you can pick and choose when you do things. So, somebody might say 'we want you to come and visit our business or local hospital or village fair on Saturday, so you visit the village fair on Saturday, then visit the

business or pop into the local hospital on the way there or back'".

"There's no point being an MP unless you enjoy people and you enjoy that sort of lifestyle. You can't go to work and go home and forget about the job. You may want to do emails or there may be an emergency in your constituency. So, like your local vicar, you respond to peoples' needs. You are there to serve your constituents".

The job isn't always what it seems

Jo Swinson: "It is a hugely enjoyable job and often what people think the job is, is quite different to what it actually is. People will say that they wouldn't enjoy it because they aren't fond of public speaking. But very little of the job is public speaking, and you practice these things and get better at them anyway. It's a job where the unseen stuff, such as liaising with local groups and organisations and taking up concerns on behalf of individuals, are the bits which often take up more of your time".

"You might ask a question in Prime Minister's Questions once in a blue moon. I would encourage people who are considering it to think about shadowing MPs or speaking to elected representatives about their experiences, rather than ruling it out on a basis of what you think the job might be. If you care about issues, if you care about your community, then this is a job that can be incredibly rewarding".

Caroline Spelman: "Yes, I enjoy my job most of the time. This is a particularly difficult time in politics at the moment, because the country is very divided, due to the Brexit issue. That has unleashed other frustrations and discontents, which are often directed at politicians. During my 21+ years as an MP, there have been good and bad times. It's like a vocation, I felt called to do it, particularly in the beginning, to put the trade injustice right, and then you're drawn into other injustices that also need putting right".

"There is satisfaction in righting a wrong, but of course there is a lot of frustration in things you can't do anything about. And this is a difficult time for MPs, because we ceded our responsibility to decide about Brexit, through the Referendum, to the electorate, and so we feel disempowered. I'm a Remainer, so it's hard for me to put something through that I fundamentally think can harm our economy. But that's what I'm bound to do by an Act of Parliament".

Pursuing your own causes
Caroline Spelman: "The first cause that brought me into politics was trade injustice. I wouldn't dream of single-handedly claiming the credit for it, but the fact is that there are now no subsidies on sugar and other pre-subsidized agricultural productions. So I'm pleased about that. I became Shadow International Development Secretary early on and I secured an annual debate on trade justice in Parliament. So I've continued to pursue the issues that I'm passionate about".

"For 14 years, I was on the front bench, so inevitably there you have to pursue the subject areas that you're made responsible for, which were health, then international development, then local government, then I became party chairman, then back to local government, and finally environment, as Cabinet Minister, which I am equally passionate about. Then when I returned to the back benches, I asked myself the question 'right, so what focus should I have for my vocation now?'"

"You'll find that when you're a senior backbencher, you can take on a lot of the less popular causes, because you've built enough capital for causes where there isn't huge support. I do a lot of work now on behalf of refugees. So as part of the immigration debate, there is not a lot of sympathy towards refugees, but most of them are fleeing dangerous environments and coming here and seeking safe haven".

"They don't have a voice, they don't often have somewhere to live. They are not in any way empowered by our democratic system, they can't vote, and so on. So I've taken up quite a lot of issues on their behalf, including things like their right to work, access to English language learning, which is problematic, and you know just trying to speak a bit of truth into a very, very toxic debate around immigration.

Predominantly, it's the men who are free to get up and move, because the women are bowed down with their family responsibilities and don't have the resources to travel. It is difficult, in International Development, we always said 'poverty often has a woman's face'. So it's those sort of issues that I've concentrated on now".

A refuge for domestic violence
"We've set up a refuge for women who are victims of domestic violence, that cause started pretty early on. Six weeks into my tenure as an MP, the police superintendent invited me down to the police station. He was a really nice man, he'd grown up on the local council estate, and he said: 'You know, Caroline, there is something you could do for us, we have nowhere to send the women who come fleeing to the police station, in fear of their lives. We have to send them back to where they've come from, which is the most dangerous place for

them to return to. We don't have a refuge here in Solihull, this borough of 200,000 people'".

"So I said: 'OK, right, I'll take that on, we'll try and get one built', and we did, and so now we have one".

"So, I started this campaign 22 years ago, it's about domestic violence, it's still a taboo subject, there was no national helpline for victims of domestic violence. This photo was of my kitchen all mocked up and we produced enough of these posters for every GP surgery and library in the country. Because one of the highest incidences of domestic violence is around Christmas time, due to the pressure and the family being thrown together. So I set up a charity called MABL (Make a Better Life). We were the prototype vehicle for the creation of a women's refuge, although Women's Aid in the end stepped in and they provided the lion's share of the funding and they now run it".

"In this country, the police receive a call every minute of every day about domestic violence. One in four women in Britain will experience domestic violence at some time in their lives. Every week, two women in the UK die at the hands of their partner or former partner".

£66bn annual cost of domestic abuse

As part of a new draft bill on domestic abuse[15] (January 2019), research estimates that this crime costs the UK economy a staggering £66bn each year. Two million people aged between 16 and 59 told the Crime Survey for England and Wales that they had been a victim of domestic abuse. This included 1.3m women and 695,000 men. For the first time, non-physical and economic abuse are to be included in the first legal definition of domestic abuse as part of a landmark overhaul of the law.

Campaigners think that this will ensure that domestic abuse gets taken more seriously, since it will be seen to have a direct impact on the economy rather than just being viewed as a 'domestic' issue. The name of the crime should be changed too.

Caroline: "One refuge is not enough, we are still short of spaces, but it was a major achievement to get a state-of-the-art refuge up and running in a borough of 200,000 and to change a bit of public expectation. It may surprise you that in the early days, people didn't like to talk about domestic violence, and they still don't like to talk about it, or think that it doesn't happen here".

"It's also interesting that the locals wanted the refuge to be just for locals, and I said 'no, it doesn't work like that, because we may have a victim of domestic violence who needs to move hundreds of miles away to be safe and we need to make our beds available to other victims who need to move hundreds of mile away from where they live, that's how refuges work', but they got there in the end, bless them. This is the point to any woman contemplating this career. Do it because you want to make a difference".

Lisa Cameron: "Two things I have initiated: one was leading on the Ivory Bill for the party, the ban on ivory was something I had spoken on and championed since I arrived. So, seeing it through the different stages of Parliament, through committee, and just the other week through the third reading as well. Seeing it happen makes me very proud. Not because there are many elephants in my constituency, but because it's historic to be a part of that and because it's such a force for good that that bill has happened".

"And the other thing I am responsible for is Chair of the Dog Welfare All-Party Parliamentary Group, for Lucy's Law, which is a ban on third-party puppy sales in pet shops. The government advice is that you should always see the puppy with the mum, but there is no ban on third parties selling puppies, which really exacerbates the puppy farming industry".

"We've had this campaign since December, and the other week on ITV News, Michael Gove agreed that it was the right thing to do and that he would be implementing it. So that's going to be coming forward as well now, as legislation. So one of the key joys of being an MP is pioneering pieces of legislation that you're passionate about, you can really make a difference".

The lows of being an MP

"Why Becoming an MP Can Ruin Your Life"
– *The Spectator*, 8th Sept 2018[16]
The Palace of Westminster is an intriguing, seductive warren of underground corridors, hidden niches, towers, and many rooms, large and small, full of drinks and canapés. As Heidi Allen said: "The place is like treacle and if you aren't careful, it will suck you in". Westminster is affectionately known as Hogwarts, and it is one of the most famous parliaments in the world. It seems specially designed for skullduggery and secrecy.

As Winston Churchill once said, "we shape our buildings and afterwards our buildings shape us", which may explain why Parliament is such a dysfunctional place. Currently, a large rebuild and restoration of the Palace of Westminster is taking place over the next five years to sort out the asbestos, dangerous electrical wiring, small fires, mice, and falling masonry.

Research carried out by Isabel Hardman[17] found that of the 666 MPs elected between 2010 and 2015 (some in by-elections), 12% got divorced whilst serving in Parliament. Of the 307 Conservatives, 32 saw their marriages end, as did 9% of Labour MPs and 12% of Lib Dems. Of the six SNP MPs elected in 2010, four split up with their spouses whilst serving. After just three years in the job, 25 of the Tory MPs first elected in 2010 were heading for divorce.

Isabel wrote: "This isn't far off the breakup rate for the general population but what is significant is how many MPs cited Parliamentary life as the cause of their problems and how quickly after entering Parliament, their marriages tend to collapse. Many affairs for married MPs start on a Monday night, when they are cooped up in Parliament waiting for late-night votes. MPs who have distant constituencies often stay in London in hotel rooms or small rented flats from Monday to Thursday and the plethora of young interns of both sexes, fuelled by alcohol and the buzz flooding round the building leads to a lot of extra-marital affairs".

She continued: "The loneliness can become apparent in other ways too, with many succumbing to alcoholism. There is a high proportion of MPs with alcohol-related problems. Charles Kennedy, the Leader of the Lib Dems was a well-known victim of drink, but there are many more. Labour MP, Liam Byrne, whose father had a drinking problem, pointed out that many of his colleagues were also children of alcoholics, which makes them more likely to develop an addiction themselves. A surprising number also come from dysfunctional families and are driven by the desire to prove others wrong, together with the seductiveness of politics and power. Becoming an MP should also come with a large warning sign: 'if your marriage isn't rock solid and your other half isn't supporting you 100% of the way, then think long and hard before standing'".

MPs are too busy being social workers to do their jobs[17]

After working in Westminster Mondays to Thursdays, most MPs journey back to their constituencies for the weekend. For some lucky ones, like Justine Greening, this will involve a short tube ride to Putney, where she has been MP since 2005. But if you are Jo Swinson, MP for East Dunbartonshire, it will be an 800-mile round trip by train (second class) with two young children under the age of four.

Many MPs grapple with the competing demands of Westminster versus their constituency. If you are young and ambitious, then climbing the slippery pole in Westminster will have its attractions, but for most of the MPs spoken with, their preference was to be in their constituency.

For many years, British politicians favoured having their main home in London whilst keeping a small toehold in their constituencies. But since the expenses scandal of 2009, where many MPs were seen to be profiteering from their London residences, things have now reversed. Several MPs such as Jess Phillips, Johnny Mercer, and the former MP Jo Cox have tried alternative and imaginative types of accommodation, including a VW campervan, a small motor cruiser, and a Thames Barge moored on the river.

Life back in the constituency involves a weekend of surgeries, local visits, and meetings. This is the right thing for MPs to be doing, to better understand the lives of those whom they represent. But there is a growing concern that the balance of responsibilities between Parliament and constituency has swung heavily towards the latter. MPs can become glorified councillors or social workers, unable to properly hold the government to account or influence national policy.

Four key issues with the British public
The four most common recurring themes that come up in MPs surgeries nationally are planning, housing, immigration, and benefits. Unlike most other jobs in the UK, MPs have no job description, require no qualifications, and have no appraisal system as to whether they are doing a good job or not, other than at the ballot box every five years.

Julie Jowit (journalist) sat in the background of a constituency surgery one weekend and watched a number of constituents who should have been trying other options. One was about planning, where the constituent should have gone to the Council, there were a number of parents with child-related school issues where they should have seen the head-teacher, a woman seeking refuge, a disabled man seeking benefits...each encounter involved the writing of at least one letter, even though few of the issues raised were matters for which the MP has most obvious responsibility or influence. And there are hundreds more requests from ordinary citizens via phone, letter, and email each week.

MPs have become short-cuts to avoid bureaucracy
More recently, an MP has often become the short-cut past other organisations with faceless and dysfunctional bureaucracy. Desperate people want a named, friendly person they can go to, and sadly, most benefits offices, Jobcentres, immigration offices, Citizens Advice Bureaus, and local government offices have become increasingly remote. To cut back on costs, victims are told to go to websites or to hold

interminably on phone lines to call centres, who won't give out names of staff over the phone. This is always assuming a victim can afford a phone in the first place.

The result is that MPs can get bogged down in constituency work to the point that they haven't got time to properly scrutinize the legislation going through Parliament, which is supposed to be their prime function. Backbenchers talk of working 50 to 70 hours a week, with about half of it on constituency case-work. Each MP receives about £120k to spend on staff, but this isn't a lot when some MPs are dealing with caseloads of 1,000 plus per annum. Most MPs spoken with had five or more staff, so doing the maths, their staff salaries would be around £20k pa, which may be enough to live on in a northern constituency, but certainly is not enough to live on in London, without subsidies from richer parents or partners.

Many MPs still use undergraduate students of politics to provide free extra labour in return for work experience during holidays. Most Parliamentary assistants are from the same stable: middle class students with an interest in politics, though refreshingly they are a diverse bunch, many from overseas.

Trolling
Justine: "I've been lucky in that I haven't had as much trolling as I know others have. I do get some, but it doesn't bother me too much. I care about what I'm doing, how my community is doing and the people I know. After that, I know the voices I hear on Twitter may or may not be representative of what most people think".

"We follow up all death threats with the police, because they are kind of serious (laughs)! But in a sense, somebody feeling threatened by the fact that you're saying something makes me just more likely to do it again. It doesn't bother me, because I know it's designed to make me think twice before saying that thing again, so it makes me more likely to shout even louder. It's an opinion, and the way that people choose to express whether they agree with you or not is at the ballot box. The way I express whether I agree with someone is through debate, not through an attack on someone just because they have a different view. I mean, god, that's not a healthy place for Britain to be in at all".

What is being done to stop the trolls?
Heidi Allen gained much publicity for showing emotion with tears running down her cheeks in the Chamber during the debate about universal credit with Frank Field on December 6[18] 2017. It was a tour de force, "but then [she was] trolled heavily afterwards. I'm not sure you can stop the trollers. I mean, the PM has tried very hard, looking at abuse and harassment in public life and asking the social media companies to do more. But the internet has just unleashed communication, hasn't it? And so often these people, they don't have photographs, they don't have names, they will have some angry symbol or letters. You can sit in a bedroom in Guadeloupe, banging away at a keyboard, and who's going to find you?"

"When it comes to death threats, I've had a few, they're in another league, and Parliament does respond differently then. We have a security team at the House of Commons. I didn't used to report things, but there was one a couple of months ago – which a number of us got, but you can only see your own name on the email – from somebody sending a hang rope. I

154

usually instantly delete, but then you think about it for a bit and you think, 'that's not on'".

"The police were brilliant, they can track people down to Google or Yahoo or whatever, and they tracked down this bloke. He was some 72 year old from the North somewhere. He was charged with harassment via electronic communications, or something like that, so it can be done".

Sarah Wollaston: "I was talking to one of my colleagues a couple of years ago about the mail I had received and she looked and said 'at least you don't get the racist stuff', which she does, and she was showing me some of hers and I thought 'my god, imagine having to cope with that as well!'"

"It is quite tough. I had a bunch of people turn up at my constituency office and leave a coffin effigy outside my door. I was with my daughter, Christmas shopping, when I found it and had to explain to her why someone had done this. That's upsetting for her and it upset me because she was with me. It's part of that wider picture, like it's coming from a wide angle sometimes, but I don't get anything like as much as some colleagues do. I reported the coffin incident because it is upsetting when it comes from your political opponents, and because they should know better. But after a couple of weeks, you just move on. You do have to be robust, because you get quite a lot of flack face-to-face as well".

"But the Parliamentary Assessment Board is good at preparing people for that, because they stick you in a room with someone being very angry at you. They stuck us in all sorts of different situations, which are fairly reflective of what you have to deal with on a day-to-day basis. So it gives people the opportunity to think 'no, I don't think I can deal with that, so maybe this isn't for me'".

Anneliese: "I've been lucky so far, probably because I was an MEP, I got used to a lot of negative comments on social media. The European debate was so polarised then and still is, so coming into Parliament in June, I was already used to it. I haven't had as much unpleasant sexist stuff as a lot of my colleagues have and I think that's because I've not had such a high profile on gender issues. Whenever I speak on national TV, then there's a bit of a spike. Some of this is fair enough if people don't agree with me, but when it's going on about my appearance, that's not relevant".

Sexual harassment – who do you complain to?
Rosie Duffield: "Labour are getting better at this and we've done a lot of work on this recently. The Women's Parliamentary Labour Party have insisted that it's an independent person that people can go to in confidence. The Speaker has set that up for the whole House as well".

On 2nd November 2017, Kelvin Hopkins, aged 76, MP for Luton North since 1997, was suspended by the Labour Party following allegations made against him, which were still being investigated one year on. According to the *Daily Telegraph*, Hopkins had allegedly sexually harassed and behaved inappropriately towards a Labour Party activist, Ava Etemadzadeh, aged 27. The claims were originally brought to the attention of Rosie Winterton in 2015 when she was Labour's Chief Whip. Hopkins has "absolutely and categorically" rejected the accusation of sexual impropriety.

Just over a week later, on 10th November, the Labour MP Kerry McCarthy said that Hopkins had been paying her unwanted attention via written notes since 1994, when both were chairs of adjacent Constituency Labour Parties in Luton. The attention resumed when McCarthy became an MP in 2005 and continued until early 2016. The notes were shown to the Labour Whips and have been reproduced in the *Guardian*. While Hopkins had not been physically abusive towards McCarthy, she told the newspaper's political editor, Heather Stewart, that "I was really, really wary of him".

In March 2018, there was outrage amongst Labour MPs when Kelvin was given permission to cross-examine her in written questions at a disciplinary hearing. Jess Phillips said she was going to cut up her Labour membership card if this was allowed to happen. Twelve months on, that disciplinary meeting has still not taken place and there is no set date for the meeting. He's not a Labour MP anymore, because the Whip has been withdrawn, but he still has his paid job as a sitting MP. Both he and his two alleged victims are complaining about the time taken for this issue to be resolved.

In July 2018, the BBC issued a story about Kelvin[19] together with a suitably victimized photo of him under the title "I want to clear my name", where he complained of the stress and intrusion to his family. There was no attempt to portray the stress and intrusion to his alleged victims, Ava and Kerry. The BBC is quick to uphold alleged perpetrators as victims of "witch-hunts" whilst their alleged victims never get equal coverage. Perhaps this is because the BBC has its own history of tolerating mass sexual predators like Jimmy Saville.

Kelvin has been suspended. So, in terms of a process for any future victims of sexual harassment, is anything being worked out? Jess: "Yes, there is a better process now in the Labour Party, but it's by no means the best process and it's not the one that we want. It needs to be completely independent in order to stop political friendships, which we all know exist, and I don't know why we feel the need to deny them".

Five-point plan to tackle sexual harassment in the workplace
Jess: "The Labour Party has tried harder than the others to get the process better. Ironically, Parliament produced a five-point plan to tackle sexual harassment in the workplace[20] for all companies in Great Britain, but whether this actually gets applied to Parliament itself, which appears to be above the law, is a moot point".

When the #MeToo movement hit Westminster in 2017, some didn't see what all the fuss was about. Those who had put their names to complaints of sexual harassment were presented as over-privileged women operating in elite institutions. If we were miffed by the odd indecent proposal or the occasional lunge from a politician, perhaps we needed an education in real suffering.

Sadly, when a woman (Jasvinder Sanghera) sought justice on harassment, the House of Lords closed ranks.[21] According to Jasvinder, Lord Lester had groped and harassed her and promised: "If you sleep with me, I will make you a Baroness within a year".[22] He then allegedly threatened to retaliate when she refused. Lester denied all the allegations, though an investigation by the Lords commissioner for standards found against him. The investigation was further scrutinized by two committee reviews, both of which found against Lester. Overall, two Law Lords, two former Lord Chancellors, the former chair of the EHRC, and 15 other peers examined the case and ruled in Sanghera's favour, but according to Lord Lester's friends in the House of Lords, this was not good enough.

Lester's friends were allowed to testify on his behalf, stating what a decent man he was and that they were concerned that Lester was being tried on the balance of probabilities, which is all that is required in a civil case. Lester was facing suspension from a job, not a prison sentence. In rejecting that standard of proof, the Lords showed that it expects to be held to lower professional standards than any other place of employment. Is this acceptable in the 21st century?

Social media and Twitter
In May 2016, Jess Phillips helped to launch a campaign called #Reclaimtheinternet, which was a cross-party effort aiming to tackle the huge amount of online abuse that women have to endure. Within hours of the launch, Jess received over 600 messages threatening to violently rape her. She complained to Twitter using the public process (the report button available) rather than as an MP to see how the general public were treated. Twitter informed her: "We reviewed the content [of your rapey abuse] and determined that it was not in violation of the Twitter rules". Jess later stated: "Twitter was colluding with abusers".

Two years later, is that still the case? "Yes, definitely. All social media and in lots of ways print media, but I find it less so with news broadcasting. There is a terrible collusion by social media companies that is damaging our democracy with false information and allowing the idea that free speech means that any idiot can say anything, whether it is true or not, and it can go round the world in seconds, so yes, it's terrible".

Is there any kind of legislation that can be brought in to stop this? Jess: "Yes, there's legislation around anonymity of people online, but also about disinformation, and they are trying to tackle this. I had a meeting with Facebook yesterday, for example, and they're doing a lot of work to stop disinformation going around, but they're only just waking up to it, and it's a bit late if you're Hillary Clinton. It's a bit late also for the whole Brexit debate".

"There is so much ability to use big data, to change the way people think and feel about things, and to just use lies and propaganda. I'm just not interested in the arguments being simple, life is complicated and there isn't anywhere near enough understanding of the complications of this place, and of politics generally. And there's nowhere near enough acceptance of how complicated people's lives can be".

"It isn't just 'you're a dole scrounger for this reason' or 'you're a millionaire for that reason'. It's not that simple, and I think that the art of simplicity in speaking, which is important, has come to override anything that's constructive or real". This is a valid point.

Clickbait

The media's desire for simple messages and sound bites to feed their consumers' limited attention spans – for example, Twitter's limitation of 280 characters (upped from the original 140 in 2018) – means that over the last 30 years, the media in the UK has dumbed down their arguments and reduced the number of syllables in their words to match the reading age of a 12 year old. Interestingly, just as the nation has become better educated, trained, and more intelligent than at any other time in history, our media seems to have gone the other way.

Jess Phillips: "Things aren't simple, and it's easy in a time when you just want clickbait, when you just want people to click on it because it'll get you advertising revenue or whatever. It's easy to say 'MPs scrounge on expenses', then list that I get whatever it is, £180,000 in expenses. I don't get a penny of that, it's to pay for my staff. It's to pay for the people who are helping disabled people get through their tribunals. But that's not what people see. They think that I get £180,000 on top of my salary".

"Why it might happen that you don't vote for something that you totally believe in… it isn't because you hate the disabled that you missed that vote, it might be for a million reasons in our democracy that don't make sense to people unless you're here. And that is the fault of the establishment, but it's also the fault of the people who report on the establishment. Politics probably always was an angry fight, but it wasn't quite so omnipresent as an angry fight in an age of social media and 24-hour news coverage. I am never away from the anxiety of what will come next: you can't turn off and I can't switch off. And it has become much more personal rather than an attack on policy or peoples' opinions, it has become a personal attack, and that is maybe more if you are a woman".

"So, I get a huge amount of very personalized attacks that have got nothing to do with what I think about welfare policy or the Home Office or my view on immigration. It's never about that, it's always about the fact that people hate me personally or love me personally, and that is the strategy that people use who wish to destroy politics. It's about division, it's about what is different about us, whether that's our race, our sexuality, our gender, there has been so much confusion in order to divide people and make people hate each other, and I'm just not interested in hatred".

Do ethnic minority women have it tougher?

Chi Onwurah: "I think it's true that we do. Diane Abbott is the MP who has received the most social media abuse and for a period in 2017, I was the MP who received the second most abuse on social media. Black women are particularly liable to be targets of social media abuse and particularly liable for it to be racist, sexist, and threatening. We need to do much more to make it clear that that's not acceptable".

"We have someone to report it to, but they can't do very much. Facebook and Twitter are doing a little more, but they are not responding to what I would call the industrialization of hate on social media. So technology gives many opportunities for communication and many positive benefits, but it also allows for the automation and industrialization of hatred. And what the social media giants are doing is not responding to that in any coherent way or using anything like the resources that they apply to, for example, advertising targeting".

Diane Abbott was more abused than any other female MP during the 2017 election.[23] Research by Amnesty International shows she received almost half of all the abusive tweets sent to female MPs in the run-up to the general election. The Shadow Home Secretary, who temporarily stood aside during the election campaign for health reasons (and no wonder!), came up against a relentless campaign of racist and sexist abuse in the weeks before the 8th June poll. The abuse directed at her amounted to ten times as much as was received by any other female MP. Whether you agree with her political views or not, there is simply no excuse for this treatment in an advanced civilization in the 21st century.

Amnesty researchers found that Abbott received 45% of all abusive tweets sent to female MPs in the six weeks before election day. In the previous six months, she received just under one-third of all abuse sent to the same group. Black and Asian female MPs received 35% more abusive tweets than their white colleagues even when Abbott was excluded from the total".

Other female MPs who received a high volume of abuse included Emily Thornberry, Angela Rayner, Joanna Cherry, and Amber Rudd, who were also in the top five targets for abuse in the six weeks prior to the snap election. Jess Phillips and Anna Soubry were also on the receiving end of the most abuse during a wider period of analysis between January and June. Thornberry said she believed the level of abuse had risen because of the number of high-profile media appearances she had done throughout the election campaign.

Measures being undertaken by Facebook and Twitter
Facebook has introduced new measures to help protect people from cyber bullying and harassment online. Individuals can always un-friend or block someone, and severe attacks that directly engage a public figure are not allowed under Facebook's latest anti-bullying policy (October 2018).

Nick Clegg, who was appointed Communications Chief of Facebook in January 2019, said they will tackle misinformation in the run-up to the EU elections in May, with a new "war room" based in Dublin. "Facebook will work closely with lawmakers, election commissions and others to fight against fake news and voter suppression efforts". Their teams will work across Facebook, Instagram, and WhatsApp.

In October 2017, Twitter brought in some measures, including more proactively banning content that glorifies or condones violence, instead of simply drawing the line at actual threats of violence. The company will also suspend the accounts of organisations that promote violence, and it expanded its definition of non-consensual nudity to include creep shots and hidden camera footage. However, it still does not appear to be doing enough to stop directly abusive tweets aimed at female MPs.

Pros vastly outweigh the cons

Most of the MPs interviewed for this book said that their biggest high was actually getting appointed. Many had worked for years, first winning over the selection committees of local party members, taking time off or standing down from their jobs, canvassing thousands of houses, spending lots of their own money, taking part in numerous debates, facing down aggression from the public both on and offline, keeping abreast of the key issues in their constituency, and nationally and maintaining enough energy and positive spirit to not only keep themselves together, but their grassroots team of canvassers.

That's quite an achievement for anyone. The majority of MPs are buoyed up by "every day being different", "really being able to make change in people's lives", "pursuing one's own causes, to the benefit of all", and "being an inspiration to one's children, friends and family". Few MPs mentioned any "lows" other than frustrations with the dysfunctionality of Parliament and not having enough hours in the day to do all the things they wanted. Trolling was a minor part of each MP's life and they did not let it get in their way.

References:

1.The Guardian (2017) [online]. Available at:
https://www.theguardian.com/politics/2017/feb/11/jess-phillips-mp-never-felt-scared-old-job
[accessed 30th Oct 2018].

2. *The Guardian* (2015) [online]. Available at:
https://www.theguardian.com/politics/video/2015/dec/14/knife-jeremy-corbyn-in-the-front-jess-phillips-video
[accessed 9th Nov 2018].

3. Phillips, J. (2017). *Everywoman: One Woman's Truth About Speaking the Truth*. London: Hutchinson.

4. Inter-Parliamentary Union (2018) [online]. Available at:
http://archive.ipu.org/wmn-e/classif.htm
[accessed 30th Jan 2019].

5. *The Daily Mail* (2018) [online]. Available at:
https://www.dailymail.co.uk/news/article-5808353/MPs-urge-Theresa-decriminalise-abortion-Northern-Ireland.html
[accessed 15th Nov 2018].

6. *The Independent* (2015) [online]. Available at:
https://www.independent.co.uk/news/uk/politics/conservative-mp-bill-cash-struggles-to-say-tampon-during-tampon-tax-debate-a6710126.html [accessed 1st Nov 2018].

7.Woman and Home (2019) [online]. Available at:
https://www.womanandhome.com/life/news-entertainment/what-is-the-tampon-tax-why-do-we-pay-it-and-when-will-it-finally-be-scrapped-205638/
[accessed 31st Jan 2019].

8. Parliament Official Website (2018) [online]. Available at:
https://www.parliament.uk/business/publications/written-
questions-answers-statements/written-
question/Commons/2018-10-23/182798/
[accessed 3rd Dec 2018].

9. *The Daily Telegraph* (2018) [online]. Available at:
https://www.telegraph.co.uk/news/2018/08/24/abortion-
home-legalised-government-bows-pressure-campaigners/
[accessed 20th Sept 2018].

10. Gender Pay Gap Reporting (2018) [online]. Available at:
https://gender-pay-gap.service.gov.uk/
[accessed 15th Jan 2019].

11. Women's Engineering Society (2018) [online]. Available at:
https://www.wes.org.uk/content/wesstatistics
[accessed 23rd November 2018].

12. Swinson. J. (2018). *Equal Power and How You Can Make It
Happen*. London: Atlantic Books.

13. *The Guardian* (2017) [online]. Available at:
https://www.theguardian.com/society/2017/nov/01/gender-
pay-gap-217-years-to-close-world-economic-forum
[accessed 30th Jan 2019].

14. Hardman, I. (2018). *Why We Get the Wrong Politicians*.
London: Atlantic Books.

15. BBC news website (2019) [online]. Available at:
https://www.bbc.co.uk/news/uk-46939735
[accessed 21st Jan 2019].

16. *The Spectator* (2018) [online]. Available at:
https://www.spectator.co.uk/2018/09/why-becoming-an-mp-can-ruin-your-life/ [accessed 15th Dec 2018].

17. *The Guardian* (2017) [online]. Available at:
https://www.theguardian.com/commentisfree/2015/may/27/tragedy-mps-too-busy-constituency-work
[accessed 10th Jan 2019].

18. *The Guardian* (2017) [online]. Available at:
https://www.theguardian.com/society/2017/dec/05/tory-mp-cries-heidi-allen-universal-credit-impact-speech-from-frank-field [accessed 10th Oct 2018].

19. BBC news website (2018) [online]. Available at:
https://www.bbc.co.uk/news/uk-england-beds-bucks-herts-44874601 [accessed 21st Nov 2018].

20. Parliament Official Website (2017) [online]. Available at:
https://www.parliament.uk/business/committees/committees-a-z/commons-select/women-and-equalities-committee/news-parliament-2017/sexual-harassment-workplace-report-published-17-19/ [accessed 30th Dec 2018].

21. *The Guardian* (2018) [online]. Available at:
https://www.theguardian.com/commentisfree/2018/nov/19/sexual-harassment-lords-jasvinder-sanghera-lord-lester
[accessed 15th Jan 2019].

22. Parliament Official Website (2018). [online]. Available at:
https://publications.parliament.uk/pa/ld201719/ldselect/ldprivi/220/22002.htm [accessed 10th Jan 2019].

23. *The Guardian* (2017) [online]. Available at:

https://www.theguardian.com/politics/2017/sep/05/diane-abbott-more-abused-than-any-other-mps-during-election [accessed 5th Dec 2018].

Chapter 8

Practicalities: The Working Week, Family Support, and Handling the Kids

So, what do MPs actually do?

A quick look at the MP's Outside Interests Report[1] shows that MPs mostly spend Mondays to Thursdays in Parliament and travel back to their constituencies for the weekend, returning to Westminster by Monday morning. Proceedings do not start until 3.30pm on Monday afternoon.

The report also gives a typical day in the life of a backbench MP in Westminster, which consists of participating in Parliamentary debates, attending and speaking at All-Party Parliamentary Group (APPG) and select group meetings, bill committees, telcons and liaison with Westminster and constituency office staff, managing both teams, budget planning, and meetings with all types of people including Whips, journalists, lobbyists, charity managers, other MPs/ministers, VIPs, civil servants, and constituents.

An MP's day back in her constituency involves two to three hours of holding a surgery with local constituents, which covers all types of issues under the sun. MPs also visit local schools, companies, hospitals, and other places of interest. The MP's staff will sort through emails, post, Twitter, Facebook, and other social media and keep up to date with news and special interests.

The job changes if you become a Cabinet Minister, though with a total of 650 MPs in the House of Commons, it takes on average 3.5 years of experience to become a Minister of Cabinet rank. (although just one year to be a Whip!). A quick look at a Junior Minister's day in the same report shows a day of back- to- back meetings in the Minister's office, the Secretary of State's office, the Departmental Office, BBC studios, the House of Commons, public dinners, after-dinner speeches, and finally the Red Box paperwork to do at 11pm each night when you get home. And this is just a Junior Minister. Cabinet Ministers barely get time to go to the toilet, let alone think strategically. Gone are the days when Disraeli used to work in the morning and spend the afternoons strolling in his gardens at Hughenden Manor.

Working week

How long is the working day – Monday to Thursdays?
Anneliese: "The working days tend to be quite long, but I don't mind that particularly, because when I'm away from home, I feel I should make use of the time as much as possible. And then when I'm back home, quite often my constituents are very understanding, and I'll say I have an event on a weekend and ask 'is it alright for the children to come with me?', and often they'll say yes".

"But it does mean that when I'm here in Parliament, I think 'right, I need to get as much done as I possibly can', because I'm well aware that my partner is looking after the kids at home, so if I was out enjoying myself, I'd feel a bit guilty!"

Sarah Wollaston: "It varies, there will be some weeks when it will feel overwhelming. It's also about coping with all the background reading and getting under the skin of the issues you're dealing with. So the background reading for the Select Committee enquiries is huge. And then of course there' is the work you do in your constituency, which of course is the key part of your role".

"You may have roles in Parliament that you want to develop, but fundamentally, your main role is representing your constituency. So in my constituency, for example, Storm Emma brought down a major communications link, and it was a huge issue. So if something like that happens, you have to drop everything and get on with the serious work of squeezing money out of the government to fix it".

"That's one of the rewarding parts of the job, because you've got to get your teeth into going to see the transport secretary, ask questions in PMQs, and someone gives you £2.5m. But it's about trying to coordinate all the evidence and get it all on the transport secretary's desk and make your case. And that's a very rewarding thing, an immediate thing. You can follow that up by going to visit the people who have been affected and their businesses. And there are a lot of other things that surround an MP's work, but if you talk to any MP, everyone does it differently. It's a great job".

Heidi: "I have no idea, I've never thought about it. Even before you get up, you have your phone going, so it probably starts about 7am each morning. I try and get home when I can, but I normally stay in London during the week. Monday is the late one usually, I normally finish up about 11.30pm at night. Tuesday, I'll try and finish a little bit earlier, normally around 9pm, and same on Wednesday. Thursday I normally have as my stay-at-home day, to catch up on paperwork, so that's normally a 7am till 7pm or 8pm sort of day".

"Friday is constituency day, so that can be a few less hours, but I'm driving between appointments and some days I might have seven, starting in the morning and I'll still be going in the evening. Saturdays, I might have a surgery in the morning and some event on Saturday afternoon. Sometimes I try and keep

Saturdays precious for emails, tweets, and journalists interviewing me. It's pretty much 24/7. A journalist will think nothing of calling you at 1am in the morning if they want you on the Today programme the next day".

Are late-night votes capped at 10pm in practice?

Heidi: "Late-night votes are supposed to end by 10pm, but some go on till 1am. It doesn't happen very often, it's to do with different types of legislation that have got protected time. Finance, or if it's a big thing like whether we're going to go to war in Syria or something like that. Some of those debates have no time limit on them, and they will continue until every person who wants to speak has had their say. Normally, the last vote on a Monday is 10pm, but about a dozen times since I've been here (every three months or so), it overruns and the latest has been about 2.30am".

Criticism from constituents

Kate: "It's a hard job with long hours, but that's not what your constituents think. They think it's quite easy. Everyone is telling me they could do it, so I keep suggesting they try. You get a lot of aggression on the job. People say 'it looks like an easy enough job to me', or 'I could do it better than you', and I think 'come and give it a go', and in fact I do say 'go and stand for election then and see if you can get elected'".

Energy

Kate: "You need phenomenal energy. Years ago, I remember being asked 'what's the best attribute you bring'? And I said I'm very energetic. I have lots of energy, physically and mentally I can keep going. I'm lucky, that's not a skill, that's something I have as an attribute".

Lisa: "Working in the NHS is good training for being here, because of the hours and because you're always doing extra things, your family is used to you being out all the time. I would say the benefit is that during the recesses, I can spend more time with my children than if I was still working in the NHS. So there are things that balance it a bit. I try and have some family days each week during recess, to do motherly things like picking the kids up and dropping them off, going shopping together, normal things that families do".

"You could spend your whole recess in your constituency office working, if you so chose. It's a job where in order to get a work-life balance, you have to work that out yourself. Nobody tells you how to do that, I know when I started in 2015, two of my colleagues were working non-stop and making themselves unwell".

Handling the kids

Anne Milton: "I had four children and my youngest was 9 when I got elected. They were aged 9, 12, 18, and 21. But primary-age children is a good time to go into Parliament, because your family is movable, it's a really good age. You need support at home, so that can be either a partner, or, if you want to pay for somebody to live with you, you can. I was lucky because my husband had a job that didn't take him far away from home and he gave up two days of work a week to support me and help with school, sports, and all the hundreds of other issues that arise with children. But as I say, no different from any other jobs that pay £75k a year".

Anneliese: "I'm lucky because although my partner works full-time as well, he stays in Oxford all the time, so he looks after the kids, and we also have some paid help as well, which we really couldn't do without and I'm very grateful for that. It's good being an MP because you have an incredible salary (£75k in 2018) which means that if you have a problem, you can deal with it. Childcare problems arise for everyone, but if you struggle to make ends meet, then it's a bigger challenge. It doesn't mean that if one of the kids is sick it isn't a problem, but it does mean that we have the means to do something about it, whereas a lot of people don't".

Dashing back and forth

Anneliese: "I initially thought I could dash to and from Oxford, but we're currently scrutinising everything as much as possible, keeping the pressure on at every stage, so we're frequently having late votes and debates. So initially I thought I could do it, because there's a bus that runs through the night back to Oxford, but getting home at midnight or 1am and then the kids waking up at half six or 7am, I realised that that's a recipe for a nervous breakdown. So normally I manage to go back on a Thursday afternoon. I've been doing a few Bill Committees recently, so that kind of pushes it back a bit on Tuesdays and Thursdays, but I normally get back by Thursday evening, so I have Friday, Saturday, and Sunday back in the constituency, which is good".

Jess: "I've got a husband! My husband has always really been the person who managed stuff anyway, because he was a night shift worker so he managed things during the day. I was always the person who was out more of the day. In that sense, it hasn't really changed that much. Although he had to stop being a night shift worker because he doesn't need to look after the children in the night. My eldest son is 13, nearly 14, so he can look after himself now. He can get himself to and from school. And my mother-in law-lives round the corner. It's a bit like *Bread*, we live on the same three streets that we've always lived on".

"So my mother-in-law picks my younger son up from school every day and takes him home and gives him tea, and then my husband will pick him up. But my husband can take him to school every day and I do every Monday, most Thursdays and Fridays, I'll take him to school, and I try and pick him up once a week, usually on a Thursday. But, yes, you just make it work, I don't think it's that difficult. It's quite a lot harder for people, perversely, whose children are in London".

"Because I do a 40-hour week in three days whilst I'm in London, I don't have anywhere else to go, so I'm just at work all that time, so I would never leave work on a Monday or a Tuesday before 8 or 9 o' clock at night. Because why would I? What am I going to do, go home and sit in a flat on my own? I mean, I get home and watch *Love Island,* but other than that, I've nothing else to do. So I just work from 9 in the morning till 9 or 10 at night every day, when I'm in London. So, it would be harder for the London-based MPs in that regard, because we're here until 7pm voting, and then they're going to get home and their kids will be in bed. I think it's probably quite hard actually if your kids are in London".

"My kids would want to see me at teatime and they'd have those expectations. I suppose they could come in here, but they'd get bored easily. So, I'm doing Mondays to Wednesdays here, and then go home. Although sometimes I'll be here on a Thursday, if there's an important vote".

Jo: "I take my four-year-old son back and forth to Scotland each week on the train. Yes, and the (impending) baby is about to make that more, we'll go back in time, I mean it's all about the iPad now with my son, whereas when he was a baby, it was all about food, so there are different ways of dealing with it".

"It's easier doing it with a 3 or 4 year-old, if they're fairly well behaved. But you have more freedom with a baby because travelling late at night, they'll sleep, whereas travelling with a toddler, you don't want to be getting a flight much after 5pm, because you're then getting home after 8pm and they're then in their massive grumpy phase. Whereas babies haven't got those kinds of patterns formed, they're happy if you've just got milk for them".

Coping with two school-aged children and commuting back and forth to Scotland

Lisa Cameron; "Without my husband, I wouldn't be able to do it. I'm part of the Speaker's Diversity and Inclusion Group in Parliament and I've been highlighting that for some sectors of society, perhaps people who are on their own with children, I'm not sure how they would manage to do this role. But they shouldn't be excluded, because they have the right to be here, to give a voice to people in their situation. There are so many challenges in Parliament to overcome, for all sectors of society to be able to be represented".

"My children are staying up in Scotland because it just isn't feasible to bring them down. I did look at it when I was first elected in 2015, but my youngest daughter was only one, so it was a real struggle for me in terms of being apart from her, and I thought about relocating the children down here, but we work till like 9pm or 10pm at night, so I'd be coming home, they'd be in bed asleep, and they wouldn't see me and I'd be leaving the next morning to come back here and then I'd have to be in the constituency hundreds of miles away at weekends, whereas they'd still be in London at weekends, when I would have been able to have more time with them. It's not really feasible".

"My husband is looking after them in Scotland. He was elected last year as an SNP Councillor, but his hours are quite flexible. There is a nursery down here, but the nursery hours don't follow the Parliamentary hours. The nursery closes before the debates finish, so that doesn't really work out either. In 2015, the nursery was closing at 6pm, which is not helpful if votes go on till 10pm. I think for staff here, it' is fine, but not for MPs, it's not flexible enough".

Challenging the 9am-6pm nursery hours culture

Lisa: "I've tried to challenge this a few times and others have as well. It's also the issue with the nursery, for instance, my youngest daughter is now four, so she could attend that nursery, but the Scottish school holidays are at different times from the English school holidays, so they're already on holiday just now, so they could come down and she could maybe be in nursery for some of the time, but then you can't access it unless you're there all year. They can fill all the places with full-timers, so why give themselves extra work by allowing part-timers? So it's not really been thought through in a way that makes it pragmatically accessible for MPs. Also, the Westminster nursery here is quite expensive in comparison to the cost of childcare in Scotland".

"I've seen quite a few of my colleagues down here with their children this week (half-term) and the children are just following them about, in and out of meetings, which shows this has not been sorted out yet".

Being a single mother and travelling back and forth to Canterbury

Rosie: "As a working mother, I feel guilty all the time, that's just a fact. My kids are almost 19 and just turned 15 years old. They're more interested in their friends and girlfriends, and my parents have been incredibly helpful, so we're now based living with my parents, so I know the boys are always OK. We talk on the phone most nights, but I miss them a lot. You know it's very difficult to juggle all of that. Of course they don't really want to be with me very much, so when I go home at weekends, I'm sort of craving their attention. And it's like my sons say 'oh God, I'm going out with my friends and I'm doing this and that', so trying to get a bit of their time is difficult. They're not overly bothered that I'm not there, put it that way, but I miss them a lot".

"We have a lot of sittings on Fridays, so I'm here most of the week. I'll do my surgery on Friday, in Canterbury, so that day is always ridiculously hard, and I work on a Saturday, so I see the kids Saturday nights and Sundays, maybe if I'm lucky, and then the recess periods aren't really holidays, we're working in our constituencies. I do see them some more then, but not as much as I'd like. I'm being invited out all of the time in my constituency. I'm saying no to working on Sundays as much as I can, because that is a family day, but yes, sometimes that is really difficult".

Effect upon children of having a mother who is an MP?

Caroline Spelman: As at the date of interview, (Sept 2018), Caroline has children who are 25, 26, and 27, so she had them before becoming an MP 21 years ago, but she would have had to manage a 4, 5, and 6 year-old from the start.

"It can only be because somehow your immediate supporters have engendered the courage in you and the belief that you can do it. It's interesting that none of my kids want to go into politics. They reckon it's very hard work, they've seen it and they've seen me get hurt and they're not keen on that idea at all. But they're very political, and who knows, when they hit their thirties and they see an injustice in the workplace, like I did, and think 'oh that's not right, that needs sorting out', you know, they may then think, like mum, I suppose, 'I'm going to have to get involved to get this changed'".

"But I notice that they're quite empowered as a result of having an MP parent. And that's interesting, because before I embarked, I didn't just do this blindly without thinking 'oh there could be problems for husband and family', I asked the children of MPs, the grown-up children of MPs, what it was actually like for them. I wanted to get a feel and the key thing that came out was 'dad was always around during the school holidays, so he had time for us then, which was great'. And that's true, you are in the academic rhythm. I didn't find any children of female MPs I could ask, it was nearly always the dad who was the MP in those days".

"It doesn't mean you're completely free, but you are in charge of your diary during the school holidays, and you can do constituency stuff and still take them to the playground in the afternoon. So that was a positive. Secondly, and this is very important, you had a feeling that dad could do something about a situation, and that's so important, because children feel just as disempowered as adults when they see some horrendous thing on the TV, such as famine in Africa or some ghastly misdemeanor, and they grow up in families where the response to that is not a feeling of hopelessness but a feeling of 'right, we can do something about this', and that passes on".

179

This is something that is a real boon for a working mother, because their children can see them going out there and doing something, whatever it is. Working mothers and especially female MPs are usually more empowered than a stay-at-home mother, in their children's eyes, though not always, since some stay-at-home mothers have set up campaigns like Mumsnet, which has changed the country.

"I'm a bit careful not to criticise stay-at-home mothers, because I stayed at home with my kids for six years, but by then, I needed to go back to work. My mother stayed at home with me and became quite mentally unwell in the end, slowly. And I made a mental note to myself not to do the same. I stayed at home for six years and I was rather envious of women who are completely fulfilled by staying at home looking after their children, because it's what the children want at that age. If you're completely content with that, you're quite lucky, especially if you can afford to do it".

"There was a stage when I regretted doing politics, because my youngest child did get badly burned, and it's what Margaret Thatcher said at the end of her career, she regretted going into politics for the sake of her family. But I'm feeling less like that now, because they are adults, and I've had this wonderful reprieve of young adulthood with my children".

"Kids in their twenties still need you, it quite surprises me, and now they're adults, the whole level of conversation is completely different, much more like equals, really interesting, and I'm looking at it and thinking, actually it wasn't easy to do what I did, but we have been enriched by it intellectually and emotionally and so on, so I think I wouldn't say I regretted doing it now".

Supportive partners

Anne Milton: "I had a very supportive partner, who always said he would cut down his working week by two days if I got elected, which is what he did. You can go it alone, in many ways it could make it a bit easier because you're not so torn on your time without someone at home as well as children who want to see you. And Parliament is quite a supportive environment. When you're elected, you're one of many new people who have been elected, if you're from one of the two main parties. I found it really supportive".

Lisa Cameron: "You need a good support structure. My fear is that someone on their own wouldn't necessarily have that support backup and that's why Parliament has to shift as well, to make it easier, in terms of accessibility for people from all types of backgrounds. I honestly don't think I could be here and doing my job if I wasn't relying on my husband to do the childcare during the week. When I arrived, someone said 'oh do you have a nanny?', and I said 'no, but I've got a husband!'"

Supportive parents

Jo Swinson: "The party was incredibly helpful and my parents, my sister, and my now husband – he was my new boyfriend at the time, he was also standing (in Chippenham), so that was very much at a distance, and we'd only been together a few months when I got elected. But certainly subsequently, he has been an absolute rock. He was in Parliament for five years with me between 2010 and 2015, and I'd say the advice that Cheryl Sandberg gives about choosing your life partner being incredibly important I think is spot on! Marrying a feminist for me was essential, and so Duncan is certainly up there".

"But in the early days, when I was in my early twenties and that relationship was very new, my parents were a huge support, letting me move back home so that I didn't have to pay rent and was therefore able to take on a part-time job so that I could spend more time campaigning. To literally delivering I don't know how many thousands of leaflets, and going and knocking on doors and giving over the dining room to a campaign office, what my parents did was absolutely beyond thanks".

Work-life balance: does anyone have time for exercise?

Heidi: "No, I don't have time to fit in any exercise. Although funnily enough, I've just recently realized I need to get a grip on that. So I've decided that the way to make it happen is to diarise it. If I diarise it, then it will happen. So, I've found a lady who's a personal trainer who lives in the next village to me and we're going to do three slots a week, which are at insane times in the morning".

Kate: "I insist on being able to do exercise, I build that into my life. I go swimming three times a week. Absolutely make myself do that".

Caroline Spelman: "I'm very sporty, I was an athlete and I played county hockey and I took up horse-riding three years ago with my daughter, which is very time-consuming. And I love it – the interesting thing is it's almost better than any gym workout, because there's so much hefting involved, hay bales, heavy pails of water – and my overall fitness levels have increased. The Parliamentary job is such a long-hours culture, involving a lot of sitting and stress, that it's important that you keep up exercise. It was impossible to do as a front-bencher, you had no life. As a Cabinet Minister, a minimum of 100 hours per week, everything goes out the window, which is not healthy, but that is how it is".

This lack of work-life balance probably puts a lot of women off, because we like to have a healthy mind in a healthy body. Especially in middle age, when women are most likely to be an MP, we are more likely to put on weight than men, and we know our bodies are judged far more critically.

Caroline: "I remember saying when I was in the department, I had wall-to-wall meetings without a single break, you didn't even have time to go to the loo! You know, this kind of back-to-back face time is just exhausting, and I used to have eight hours of paperwork each day at the weekend. Boxes would arrive…. I honestly don't think it needs to be like that. It's slightly a way of controlling the ministers".

"I'm convinced there's got to be more efficient ways of dealing with that. I didn't crack it whilst I was there. I used to go and nick the stuff off the pigeon holes before it got in my red box and deal with it, so that I didn't end up sitting till one in the morning doing the red boxes, it was just exhausting. It took me a while to get over it, but I've recovered now. What's interesting is that having lost my position as a Cabinet Minister, quite often the Whips put me in touch with the ones (the ministers) that have just lost their jobs, because they feel I have navigated that change well. And indeed, I have a much better work-life balance now, and I'm enjoying it more as a consequence.

"And you know, I can work through with some of the recently sacked ministers, the stages of anger, despair, sadness, and frustration, and move on to: 'Well right, these are all the things you could be doing with your time. Have you thought about going on a Select Committee? It's a great experience, you'd bring firepower to a Select Committee, because you understand how ministers work'. And I've managed to recycle quite a few ex-ministers into Select Committee roles. It used not to be possible, but it is now".

"It isn't really the role of HR to do this, because HR is the Whip's office and the Whip's office comes with the patronage problem, so people are reluctant to tell the Whips what they really think or where they don't want anything to count against them. You know, when you need to sound off to somebody about how frustrating it was to be sacked, how discarded you feel. You don't want to say that to the Whip's office, but you could say it to a colleague who had been through it, they would really understand that".

"I have my agony aunt role, you know, it's all right! Luckily I enjoy that kind of thing, I so enjoy seeing people have a re-blossoming into new roles as former Cabinet Ministers. You can probably think of a few. It just gives me pleasure to see them flowering, having re-found their feet. The House is very forgiving. If you come back huffing and puffing and you're angry and bitter, the House can't handle that at all, they turn against you. If you come back in with good grace and you start contributing on something you know a lot about, or really care about, the House helps you with that".

Job-sharing
Caroline Lucas put forward a very good argument for job sharing in her book *Honourable Friends? Parliament and the Fight for Change.*[2] For such a full-on 24/7 vocational job, it makes a lot of sense to have two people doing it so there is coverage at all times, and it enables the other half to have holidays and some sort of home life.

Sarah Wollaston

"At the moment, there are some over-represented and some very under-represented groups, and I'd like to see Parliament help by introducing job-sharing. I used to job-share as a doctor, and it was very successful, people had two doctors for the price of one. I job-shared with a doctor who had an interest in diabetes and endocrinology and I had other areas of past experience and between us we covered a wider spectrum, and of course people could choose which doctor they saw. So if they had a diabetes issue, they could go and see Marie-Therese, and if they had another sort of issue, they could come and see me. It was a way of being mutually supportive as well and between you, you covered more hours and patients than you would as a single person".

"And we'd find the same in Parliament, that people could benefit from having a job-sharing MP who would cover a much broader spectrum. It would encourage people to apply at an earlier stage in their career, so they could then keep their career, or it could allow people with disabilities to apply. So, I could see that towards the end of my parliamentary career, I could support somebody else coming into politics and help them if they had caring commitments or whatever and they didn't feel ready to be doing it full time. So you could have that kind of partnership working. It's disappointing that these suggestions are dismissed instantly".

"Of course, it would be down to the electorate if they wanted a job-sharing MP. I get a bit frustrated that there's a kind of brick wall to anything that seems different. I'd like to see Parliament use that as one of many mechanisms to diversify what it does. Yes, we'd have to think carefully and put it to the vote, but I don't think it's beyond the wit of man or woman to work out how you could make that happen as a model".

"Caroline Lucas and I have both suggested this in the last year, and it's gone into the 'too difficult' box. But sometimes in this place, you just have to keep going. We were discussing baby leave the other day, Harriet's suggestion, who would have thought? Child-friendly hours?"

Heidi: "I think job-sharing would be hard. Not impossible, but hard because of the bouncy roller-coaster nature of Parliament, you can't get off the roller-coaster because it's Tuesday afternoon and it's not my time now. It's not a routine kind of job. So it's not to say it's impossible, but I would think it would be pretty hard. It's just that you're on all the time, there's no natural break in the week. I mean, maybe you could use someone who was more constituency-focused and someone who was more Westminster-focused, I don't know, really it's a seven day a week job".

Moving to a new building

Westminster is a decaying, Victorian building well past its sell-by date. It is affectionately known as Hogwarts for its amazing architecture, rambling corridors, and beautiful statesmanlike rooms. Eight thousand people work in Westminster with over one million people visiting it each year. There have been 60 incidents over the last ten years which could have led to a major fire. Westminster is heated by a high-pressure steam heating system that could burst at any time.

In January 2018,[3] MPs voted to support an amendment put forward by Labour MP Meg Hillier for a full programme of works (the Restoration and Renewal Programme) that is likely to result in the Commons relocating to Richmond House (another building in Whitehall) and the Lords to the QE2 centre from about 2025.

They would be off the Westminster site for approximately six years and the cost is currently estimated at £3.5bn. The remit of the Restoration and Renewal Programme is to replace everything "as is". So, this is a massive missed opportunity to re-design and innovate.

The other option put forward by Andrea Leadsom was for everyone to remain onsite and to have a programme of works fitting around the MPs and Lords. There had been much debate about whether to stay put or move everyone out and operate Parliament from some other building, either in London or around the country. In the end, the latter option of moving everyone out for six years won the vote, because the former option of working around the sitting MPs and Lords would have cost an estimated £5.7bn over 35 years, so, £2.1bn extra and a lot longer than moving people out.

This would be a great opportunity to re-design the Chamber and make it more collaborative by having a horseshoe design, along the lines of the Scottish or European Parliament, or in fact most modern Parliaments around the globe. The current Chamber is one of the few adversarial-designed Parliaments left and creates a combative approach to debate by having the government face the opposition. How childish is that? The public have been unimpressed by behaviour in Parliament ever since TV cameras were first introduced in the 1990s. It had been hoped MPs might improve with the advent of cameras, but this is not the case.

Heidi: "We are one of very few Parliaments in the world to have an adversarial setup and there are mixed views about it. The whole debate at the moment is whether they refurbish Parliament whilst we're here or we all get shipped out. I'm pragmatic, it's a place of work, it's a building. Yes, architecturally, of course it needs preserving, because it's a part of British history. But do I care particularly if we don't move back here and end up in some purpose-built modern debating chamber somewhere? Then that would suit me just fine. I refuse to be overawed by the building here. It's just a place of work. There are some who call me all sorts of unmentionable names for that and who worry that if we move out, we will never move back. I think we should do whatever is cheaper: it is the public purse".

Kate: "If we all moved out for the refurbishment of Parliament, I think it would be such a break, we'd have to learn to behave differently. We'd be in a very different setting and that would have an impact on behaviour. It would be an opportunity, exactly as you say, to set up a less adversarial environment. To design the debating chamber so it wasn't eyeball-to-eyeball, make it horseshoe-shaped. I'm probably a bit of a lone voice on this one, thinking that would be a good thing, but I do".

"Look at the European Parliament, the United Nations, the Scottish Parliament, anywhere you like really: they are more collaborative by design. I would welcome that, but I don't think I'm in the majority, even among other women, possibly".

Scottish Parliament
Lisa Cameron: "The Scottish Parliament is a new Parliament, so it doesn't have any of the history of Westminster. It started as a modern Parliament and first sat in 1999, with the new Parliament building opening in 2004, and that helps in terms of being more progressive from the start. Some of the traditions here perhaps don't align themselves to that so well. However, things are gradually changing, and I think that female MPs are really crucial to that".

"The horseshoe-shaped chamber of the Scottish Parliament makes it more consensual. Also, it's not just a first-past-the-post voting system in Scotland, there's also a list system, which includes proportional representation. So, it's quite adversarial in Westminster because you're competing, whereas with the different PR system in the Scottish Parliament, there doesn't seem to be the same sides".

What keeps MPs awake at night?
Caroline Spelman: "I like to have a clear conscience when I put my head down on the pillow, so I examine the day and try and make sure I've done the right thing, because you've got to have a bottom line in politics. If I haven't done the right thing, that will keep me awake, and I need to put it right. But the thing I worry about most is that both of the main parties are struggling with their modus operandi, as you can see".

"I've been a party chair, so I don't think they will fracture and create a new party. People always talk like that, it sells newspapers, but they definitely need to modernize. It's quite difficult at the moment to see a way forward, especially on Brexit, it does trouble me".

"It troubles me because those are people's livelihoods that are at risk, and as a result I worry about the divisions in our society that have got worse following the 2016 Referendum and whether we can heal those up. So that kind of keeps me awake at night. I also lie awake sometimes worrying about a constituent. I have a very big surgery caseload because I have a council estate of 60,000 people. It was the subject of a seminal work by Lynsey Hanley, the broadcaster, called *Estates*.[4] The Chelmsley Wood estate is just outside Birmingham and it's one of the largest estates in Western Europe. A lot of my caseload comes from there, I deal with on average about 1,000 cases a year".

"It's a big caseload, I do a four-hour surgery on either a Friday or Saturday, and we deal with a lot of email caseloads and calls as well. And we do occasionally have someone in my surgery who's in such a predicament that I don't sleep, someone who's suicidal, for example, or when a child has gone missing. You know, we have big stuff and that does affect me. I'm in a position to swing some services into action over the weekend, we have hotlines, and I sometimes do that because I think a life is at stake, and I have to act on that".

We can expect too much from our MPs. On the one hand, we expect them to be social workers in their constituencies, and at the same time to be up to dealing with complex legislation and front-bench politics. Also, they need sales skills, the ability to run an election campaign, to manage their own business and, manage two remote teams, listening skills, persistence, political cunning, a great brain, and a long- hour working ethic. That's an awful lot of skills to have in one person.

Caroline: "Expectations of MPs have got higher and peoples' tolerance of a situation that you've done your best in has got lower, and I find that difficult. I find it difficult on behalf of my casework team, because my senior caseworker has travelled the entire journey with me – well, 18 out of 20 years – and when I see or hear people being really rude to her, I get upset about that because she is class. If anyone can sort out a mess or a problem, she can. I mean, she's got infinite patience with people. We are finding that people are becoming more short-fused, sadly".

"Yes, fake news and the ability of ordinary people to send out an angry tweet is very damaging. But bless them, my constituency has very kindly returned me five times in elections. I'm not complacent about that, I was elected on a majority of just 482 on an electorate of 83,000. I will never forget that. I think the casework is the key to that. So, the most important thing is that they know I am there for them, and I will always try. I can't solve everything, but we can solve quite a lot, and we do, and I think that that counts for more than which way the political wind is blowing. I've been in opposition and in government, you know".

Heidi: "Oh, always that I haven't done enough, it's so hard. I'm an all-or-nothing person. You can't fix everything overnight in this job. When I ran my own business, I would see a problem and fix it, change something by getting a different supplier. Here, I constantly feel like I'm just bobbing on the top of a wave of an issue, like child refugees. I'm not Home Secretary, so I can't change policy, so all you can do is just 'bob', and try and pull the boat in the direction you want it to go".

"I constantly think if I hadn't spent the night doing my emails and instead written a speech about something, or another refugee camp had been visited…. I feel personal responsibility for everything I touch, if you like, and you can't, you can only do your best, or you exhaust yourself".

References:

1. UK Government website (2018) [online]. Available at: https://www.gov.uk/government/collections/mps-outside-interests [accessed 18th Dec 2018].

2. Lucas, C. (2015). *Honourable Friends? Parliament and the Fight for Change.* London. Portobello Books.

3. *The Guardian* (2018) [online]. Available at: https://www.theguardian.com/politics/2018/jan/31/mps-set-to-leave-houses-of-parliament-for-35bn-restoration [accessed 13th Nov 2018].

4. Hanley, L. (2007). *Estates: An Intimate History.* London. Granta Publications.

Chapter 9

"Equality for women demands a change in the human psyche, more profound than anything Marx dreamed of. It means valuing parenthood as much as we value banking"
– Polly Toynbee

Short-term measures to get more women into Parliament?

Sarah Childs, is a Professor of Politics and Gender at Birkbeck, University of London. She spent over two years researching and visiting Parliament, and observing gender and diversity within. She wrote the "Good Parliament" Report[1] in July 2016, which makes for fascinating reading. In it, she makes 43 recommendations for Parliament to adopt, to create a more gender equal and diverse working environment. When interviewed two years later in July 2018, she said: "there has been some good progress" on 12 out of the 43 recommendations.

She observed that all progress on modernizing Parliament is slow, on any issue, because no one person is in overall charge. It's not like a company with one CEO who can make immediate changes and has top-down power throughout the organization. Power in Parliament is devolved to many individuals and committees. There is the Speaker, the Deputy Speakers, the Leader of the House, the Chief Whip, the Clerk of the House, the Clerk of the Workings of the House, the Clerk of Standing Orders, the Clerk of Parliamentary Reform, Select Committees, and General Committees, such as the Joint Committee on the Palace of Westminster, which makes decisions on the Restoration and Renewal Programme which will go on until circa 2030; the list goes on and on.

Progress on the Good Parliament recommendations

Recommendation 3: Permit MPs to be counted at the "door" of the division lobbies when accompanied by their children. In lieu of this recommendation, in March 2017 the reference group endorsed the Speaker's approach to allowing children up to the age of five in the division lobbies and into and through the Chamber whilst a vote is underway.

Recommendation 5: Initiate an Inter-Parliamentary Union audit in 2018. Approved.

Recommendation 12: Produce a House statement on maternity, paternity, parental, adoption, and caring leave. The House passed a motion in favour of allowing members who have had a baby or adopted a child to vote by proxy.

Recommendation 13: Undertake a review for the provision of a crèche facility on the Parliamentary estate. An options review was carried out in 2017, following which an emergency childcare service is being piloted.

Recommendation 14: A rule change should be sought whereby any Select Committee witness panel of three or more must be sex/gender diverse if, by the end of the 2015 Parliament, select committees are not reaching a 40% sex/gender threshold amongst witnesses. In June 2018, the Liaison Committee recommended that "for Committees represented on the Liaison Committee, a panel of three or more witnesses should normally include at least one woman...our aim is that, by the end of this Parliament, at least 40% of discretionary witnesses should be female".

Recommendation 16: Revise the dress code to "business dress". Approved.

Recommendation 17: Recognise the House's collective responsibility for enhancing representation and inclusion by formally taking note of the Good Parliament Report. The Commission formally took note in July 2016.

Recommendation 20: Re-design the parliamentary identity pass. Implementation of the new double-sided passes began in September 2017.

Recommendation 25: Put before the House a motion to establish the Women and Equalities Committee as a permanent Select Committee of the House. Approved.

Recommendation 28: Require the House Service to provide comprehensive and systematic diversity data in respect of select committee witnesses, and establish annual rolling targets for witness representation. A breakdown of witnesses by gender is now published as part of the annual sessional return for each committee and consideration is being given to how this might be extended.

Recommendation 29: Ensure that House rules and structures, institutions, nomenclature, and culture are diversity-sensitive and inclusionary. Production of an accessible Guide to Procedure is underway and has been published on the beta website. The Procedure Committee has published proposals for gender-neutral Standing Orders, but is awaiting the tabling of the necessary motion to introduce them.

Recommendation 40: Abolish the "10-year dead" rule whereby only individuals who have been dead for at least a decade are represented in artworks in the Palace. The rule was revised by the Speaker on the advice of the Reference Group in July 2016.

It is good to see that there has been positive progress on these 12 issues, but sad to see that many of the more important ones, such as gender and diversity quotas, non-sexist behaviour, and committing to no more all-male panels, have not been achieved. There is still much work to do.

Anne Milton: "The press have got a role to play here, because there is quite negative reporting of women in the media. They focus on shoes not views, and not talking about the fact that politics is a reasonable career for women".

"If you're going to recruit more women into Parliament, it should be returners (from having children), because it's a really good career as a returner. It's something different, you've got some life experience. If you're looking for a seat, and it doesn't matter which political party it is, having children under the age of 12 is a great age to be looking for a constituency, because you can move to the patch because your family is transportable at that age, so those are the people I would recruit".

Heidi: "It's a bit difficult to engineer or manufacture solutions. It is role models, having somebody that you can talk to, that impresses and coaches you and tells you that you can do that. At my local Council elections, I've got Heather, Lina, Harriet, Ruth, Barbara, Shrobona, and Evelyn. These are all my girls coming through, at District and County level. Some got in last year and about two-thirds more are standing this year".

"When I spot somebody good, I ask them and they say 'don't be ridiculous, don't be ridiculous', so I say 'well, if you ever fancy a glass of wine, come and chat to me about it'. It's just sowing the seed and I think particularly when, like me, for example, who did it from a standing start and knew nothing about politics whatsoever, you know I only became a member of the party in 2012".

Jess: "Positive discrimination, positive action is the only thing that actually works quickly. So, all of the encouraging, the training and trying to change your culture within your political party are things that are important and the Tories do quite a lot of that.

"And maybe they do a better job of providing financial support for people, because it's quite a big job being a candidate, and there's no remuneration. So, if you've got a couple of kids and a job, it's pretty hard to do. But that said, it doesn't increase the numbers, and in fact, the Tories have gone backwards! The only thing that has ever worked is positive discrimination, all-women shortlists, and so it has to happen, there isn't any choice".

Jo Swinson: "In terms of short-term measures, all parties try to do this. They encourage more women to come forward to be candidates. You know, the campaign run by 50:50 Parliament, with the hashtag #AskHerToStand, which I think is great. That is something everybody can do, even if you don't want to be a politician yourself, you can think of somebody who would be a great councillor or a great MP, and you can put the thought into their head".

"You know, sometimes it takes a couple of suggestions, the thought just needs to nurture and lie there for a bit. The person says 'oh no, I couldn't possibly', but then it takes root, and that becomes 'oh well, maybe I could', so that's a short-term thing which I encourage people to do. My anecdotal research, speaking to women MPs, more women end up doing the job because somebody suggested it to them than men,

197

who seem to wake up one morning and think 'yeah, I'd make a great MP!'"

"So, that's a short-term thing and of course parties then rightly, and often brilliantly, put in a lot of effort to provide training, mentoring, support, not because women necessarily need more of that, although sometimes it is a more hostile environment, online abuse is greater. But it's also because you're trying to get women to outperform the numbers. If only a third of your candidates list are women and you're trying to get to 50% women MPs, then you need each individual woman to do better than each individual man. So, that is one of the reasons why parties do that, and that's important".

Kate: "We're pushing very hard at the moment for proxy voting, so that women on maternity leave, for example, can take time off to be with their baby, which doesn't happen at the moment. So better recognition of women's family responsibilities, particularly around maternity, which is unique to women, would be a good short-term signal that we can design this place to work round other commitments in your life". Baby Leave was finally passed in January 2019.

"We've made improvements on the working hours, but one of the problems with week-to-week short-termism is how hard that is for parents, particularly mothers, to plan childcare arrangements and Parliamentary life. So better certainty about our timetable would help more women with family responsibilities".

"There are lots of really good engagement programmes: Fabian Women's Network Programme, Labour Women's Network Training, the Parliament Project. We need to spread those as widely as possible. We'd get more women into politics if we had better political education in this country in our schools, in our colleges, in every aspect of society".

Order of business for each week is only announced the previous Thursday
Kate: "Every Thursday, the government announces the business for the following week and an indication of the business for the week after. Sometimes, it will only give you the scantiest of information, i.e. it may tell you what's happening on the Monday week, but not much more".

"There are some things you do know a long way in advance, but the core business, week by week, is confirmed on the Thursday for the following Monday. And that is not absolutely what's going to happen, because each day urgent statements and questions will be tabled. And that's reasonable, I'm not complaining about that, since there will be urgent business every day. Things will have cropped up, the Salisbury attempted murder for example, which created the need for an urgent statement in Parliament".

"That means that the Whip, the requirement your party imposes on you to be here at certain times, can only be confirmed the Thursday night before. That is difficult for families to plan around their other commitments. You know that you need to provide childcare all week from 9am to 5pm. The difficulties are when unexpected things happen, and the Whip is pretty rigid, so then it can mean quite a lot of difficulty with outside hours".

Rosie: "We need to talk to other women about what is involved. Try and encourage them to stand. Frances Scott of the 50:50 Campaign[2] says that you have to ask a woman three times, but you only have to ask a man once. So I think there's something we need to do about encouraging women, saying you may not feel you're perfect, but you're definitely good enough. Changing the hours here would make it easier, childcare and things like that, but that applies to men as well. I know two new male Labour MPs who have brand newborn babies and had to leave them before they were 24 hours old".

"That was incredibly difficult for both of those men. One was really emotional about it, and found it very hard. And people assume it's just women who are interested in that, but there's a great push now. The hours are horrible, some of the voting takes place in the early hours".

"Most of the debates don't go on beyond 10pm, but when we were discussing the EU Withdrawal Bill, we were here till 2am one morning and 1am another. So it's OK for me (since my children are older), but generally women are put off by that. And we know most women have the caring responsibilities, so you may have a mother or a grandmother as well as the children to look after, so we have to make it a bit more flexible".

"We're talking about things like shared parental leave and possible proxy voting: Harriet Harman's baby leave policy. But I don't see why we can't look at electronic voting in this century. That's another way forward, we don't always have to physically be here. And tackling the online abuse, that would be a good idea; we need the social media companies to take responsibility for that though".

The percentage of female Tory MPs hasn't increased since 2015 – it's still 21% – while Labour female MPs are 45% of the party. Is it time for the Conservatives to bring in all-women shortlists?

Caroline:

"I'm not a fan of all-women shortlists, based on what my female Labour colleagues have told me. It makes them feel a bit like second-class citizens in Parliament, because they got in on an all-female shortlist. And there's a backlash in the constituency because the electorate wasn't given a choice, and they resent it. David Cameron's 50:50 shortlists were good, and we made a big step from when I was selected (in 1997), when only 8% of the party was female, to 21% now, so that's progress, but we can still do more, and one of the big problems is the feed through".

"When you're getting ten men for every woman applying to be an MP, the pool that you're drawing from is smaller. Your talent pool is also smaller and a lot of women who are very capable, maybe had a real top career before contemplating a career in politics, actually look at it and they're a bit reluctant to give up what they've worked hard for. It nearly always requires a pay cut at the top level, and also the thing they don't like is intrusions into their family's private life, which I experienced, and it is terrible. Those are the big deterrents".

"The 50:50 shortlists are good and that should be systematic. If you're taking 20 to the longlist and 50% are women, then there's a good chance that you'll put through more than one. When I was doing it, I was the only woman out of 20 being interviewed, and there was nothing for them to compare me with. And you could feel that it was tokenistic. So, stick with the 50:50 shortlists, and I would like to see UK privacy laws changed to protect children. There's no privacy for children in our legal system, which I think is appalling. Their faces don't always get fuzzed out. The *Daily Telegraph* put a photo of my son on the front page when he was 15, without permission, a copyrighted photograph. They don't always ask".

"There is no law to protect children. I feel that is a gap, and other practices...if your child messes up, as poor Tony Blair knows, everyone remembers that Ewan was drunk in Leicester Square, and I think that's much more problematic for the mums, thinking about being politicians. Because you don't mind if you're castigated for your choice of clothes or something you've said, maybe it was stupid and maybe the outfit was dreadful, I had a shoe ASBO once! That's all superficial, but it isn't superficial when your child is attacked for something stupid they have done wrong, because you are always in those situations 'a top Tory', you know. As a woman, it makes it ten times worse, and I feel that the law is wrong, I would change that".

Electronic voting

Sarah: "There are other things that we used to do, top to bottom, and I remember one of my other colleagues saying to me, shortly after I'd arrived here, in the Lobby, as I was saying 'why on earth are we all spending 20 minutes trooping through division lobbies rather than voting in a much more sensible way?' and he said 'wait two years and it will all make perfect sense!' Well, I've been here eight years now and it still doesn't make sense! I would have hoped that moving out of the Palace of Westminster for the rebuild would have been an opportunity for us to explore electronic voting".

"It seems extraordinary, the waste of time and money that we spend on the physical process of voting. And if you're in the middle of a Select Committee hearing, you can be disrupting the entire hearing for over an hour whilst you're all literally physically walking through a division lobby. I can see the benefits of people being in one place, because it's a chance for people to collar ministers. But we could all be in one place in the division lobby and press a button, and then those who need to stay to catch somebody could do that. But the current mechanism is so time wasteful, I don't think we would tolerate any other public body behaving in this way".

Anne Milton: "I don't like electronic voting. Division lobbies are important places, they are the only chance you can guarantee to see other MPs. I don't think there's any MP who would like to get rid of the division lobbies. You get a chance to see ministers, MPs from other parties, and anyone else you need to see without making appointments.
It's a great place to grab a minister, grab anyone! We're voting on the laws of the land, for goodness sake, you don't want to just press a button, do you? And as I say, it's invaluable for MPs, and for me meeting opposition MPs, I can grab them too".

"There's a lot more close working between political parties than you might imagine. I wanted to see John Mann (Labour MP) the other day. I said to someone, 'if you see John Mann, can you grab him?' And at a vote, I know they'll be there. It's the one place where you know if there's a three-line whip, then everybody will be there, it's really valuable".

Conditions of selection
Caroline: "We should try anything to make it easier for people in stressful situations, or going through a stage of their lifecycle with small children or whatever. Because it was difficult for me, I had three children, and I entered Parliament with their ages six, four, and two. I don't know how we managed, somehow we did, but it was just jolly difficult, and the hardest thing was living apart. It was a condition of my selection to school my children at a state school in the constituency".

"There was a reason for that, because I was new, they wanted me to become part of the community, and as a consequence, we did, they were right, but it's very hard to live apart from small children and I pined for mine and after a year and a half, I said 'I just can't hack this, I want to have my children with me'. So I brought them all to London, but the rules say you can only have a one-bedroom flat. So my husband provided large enough accommodation for us all to live together. But it's not easy at the London end. It's not a great place to raise your kids when their mum is working till 10pm at night".

"It's still very difficult, this is what is hard, this is what puts women off applying in equal numbers, and I'd like to see that improve. I was lucky because I had a supportive husband, but he's not a house-husband". Caroline's husband is a senior partner at Accenture and is often away abroad on business, so this must have been doubly difficult for her.

Au pairs
Caroline: "You've got to have help. I was lucky, I had a string of excellent au pairs, but you still have disasters, one may go home because they are homesick. For a lot of working women, that is where the difficulty is. It's not even like you are in a 9am to 5pm job. So what's really hard is you've told the au pair that you're going to be back by 7pm tonight, and then, ten minutes beforehand, it switches to being 10pm. That makes it difficult for any working relationship and that unpredictability makes it hard for the women, with children".

"I was lucky, I had good girls, I made them a part of our family, we embraced them and took them on holiday with us, my children's recollections of the au pairs is good. They remember them, they liked them, and some were brilliant cooks, some couldn't cook at all. I couldn't have got by without some childcare, and there is now a nursery here, there wasn't when I started. But it's limited, you might not want to bring your children in. I know that my secretary was anxious about using the nursery because you're in a bit of a hot spot for terrorism, sadly, we know this, and this is still a difficult area".

"Westminster terms don't fit with school terms or Scottish terms. And now parts of the country have half-terms at different times. So, whilst there's a half-term in the spring term, the London half-term, which is what Parliament tends to respect, is the same as the West Midlands term. In the West Midlands half-term week, you'll find that the MP parents have got their children in London, shoving them round the Eye or having a tour of Parliament or doing a jigsaw puzzle in the corner, I mean it's difficult. And then during the autumn term, we don't have half-term at all. The whole Parliament is awash with MP's children, so you are juggling".

"As Harriet Harman was saying on the radio this morning (12th Sept 2018), it's ridiculous that in the 21st century, this institution has no proper maternity leave".

Caroline: "It's crazy! When you say that to the outside world that there's no maternity leave for MPs, they go 'what?' As if you're supposed to drop the baby and carry on! There's no maternity leave, there's no latitude for any family disaster. And you can have elderly parents who are poorly. I was appalled, when I came in here, to know that one of the MPs, whose wife was dying of cancer, wasn't allowed to be with her when she passed away, and he was so upset about that. I just think this is what needs to change".

If you had a magic wand, what one thing would you change about Parliament?

Anne: "I'd have it refurbished. I would put in place modern employment practices. You don't need to get rid of traditions to make it a modern workplace. You could still have your traditions, but we've done badly with putting those two things together. You could still have the State Opening of Parliament, and you could still have some of the curious language we do, but the way we do business is still very time-consuming. But I have a constituency close to London, so I am luckier than many".

Heidi: "What would I change? Some of the systems and processes are very antiquated, they're not business-like at all. And the game-playing and the pretence and the planted questions and speeches and the Whips bullying the new ones to go in there and make a speech 'and this is what we want you to say...'. I'd love to change that".

"I don't know if that is a symptom of politics or just the kind of leadership we have. This place culturally is like treacle. If you're not careful once you get in this place, it just pulls you in. I remember when we first joined in 2015, it was the 1922 Committee, which is a backbench committee which happens every week, and David Cameron came to speak to us, basically just to say 'well done everybody', and when he arrived in the room, to a man and woman, old and new, everybody started banging wood! And I'm thinking, 'what is wrong with your hands?' It's literally the culture, it grabs you and if you're not careful you become part of it".

"How you break that cycle of process, playing the game, banging wood, it's institutional almost, like boarding school. So it would take a very different leader, business-focused leader, or leaders in all the parties, and maybe moving out of here might help that".

Parliament is too London-centric
Jess: "Changes to Parliament? I would make it not be in London, that would be the one thing that I would change. It's ridiculously London-centric. All decisions made are made about an economy that doesn't exist anywhere else in the country. And even a political horizon that doesn't exist anywhere else. I am astounded by how London-centric politics is. It's not even that it's a Westminster bubble, it's a southern part of the country bubble. I hear people say things and I think 'oh my god, you have literally never lived'. The rest of the country exists, and so things would be vastly improved if they were made to go somewhere else for a bit".

Is this why so many people outside London voted for Brexit?
Jess: "Yes, because people in here don't know what they're talking about. They don't know what it's like to live in a mill town in Lancashire, it's unbelievable".

Teleporting
Jo: "If I had a truly magic wand, I would have a teleportation portal in Parliament, so the MPs could use it to get back to their constituencies. Representing a constituency that is 400 miles from London and doing an 800-mile round trip every week, that is probably my greatest frustration with the job. And it would be a significant advantage to be able to make a quick trip back to the constituency to attend something you wanted to go to, on a Tuesday night, which for me currently, it's just impossible to do that. And equally to not be travelling 800 miles a week, particularly now that I do that with one small person, soon to be two. At least I used to get a lot of work done on that commute, but those days are long gone".

No latitude for family emergencies

Caroline: "It needs to modernize, the hours are ridiculous and it's totally unnecessary. So, for example, yesterday I had a long-standing engagement, where I had promised to go and see the newborn of an au pair who used to work for me, and it was all organized when suddenly we had to sit beyond seven o' clock. And it can be worse than that, we can sit beyond ten o' clock. And the unpredictability of it is very difficult to handle in any family, because you make commitments to pick children up or you need to go to something where family needs you there, or parents' evening at school, or the child is not well. I had a bad year with this actually, that really brought it into focus".

"Whereas I thought it would be a greater challenge when the children were little, they're now adults and you think you won't face this again, but my daughter broke her femur in the winter, you know the terrible snow and ice that we had? Massive break, just below the hip joint, and you know, you have to drop everything, you are mum! And my husband works abroad, so he wasn't around to help out, so I commuted to and from Birmingham, when she first came home, which was tough. It's two hours each way and there was no latitude, and when she was just about to go into the operating theatre for surgery, I rang the Whips and said 'I can't make the 10pm vote tonight, my daughter has had a bad injury, I'm the next of kin, there isn't another next of kin or family member within 120 miles' and they said 'you have to be here'.

"So, I had to come down. She was in recovery, so I knew she'd got through the operation. It was serious because she'd been five days nil by mouth. It was a week before they operated, I came down, I got here, and there was no vote!"

"So I turned around and that's what's frustrating. I caught the 10.43pm, the last train back to Birmingham. That's tough, and then just a matter of six weeks later, my husband had a burst appendix. Emergency, blue lights to hospital, and when they wanted to discharge him, it had taken so long to get my daughter out of hospital when she was discharged that I thought 'oh no, here we go again', so I rang the Whips and I said 'the hospital wants to discharge my husband today, we've got a running three-line whip from 3.30pm today, I very much doubt that I'll be able to make the 3.30pm because it took me until 4pm last time to get my daughter out, so can I have a bit of latitude?' 'No!'"

"So, I rang my husband back and said 'you'll have to get a move on because I've got to be in London by 3.30pm', and he said 'I've got good news, I'm good to go!' I said 'what do you mean?' and he said 'someone else needs my bed!' I said to him afterwards, 'the thing is, there are not many jobs where they refuse you to be at your next of kin's bedside, but this is one of them.'"

What about informal pairing?

"There is no formal pairing. All the time I've worked here, for 21 years, there's been no pairing, they scrapped pairing in 1997. The informal pairing system failed in a very public way with Jo Swinson when she was on maternity leave in July 2018. Julian Smith, the Tory Chief Whip, asked MPs to breach Commons voting conventions[3] in knife-edge Brexit votes, as opposition parties demanded he quit and queried the accuracy of the PM's account of events. Party sources conceded that Julian Smith had asked several Tory MPs to break their pairing arrangements in order to win the vote, but most had refused to do so. The only one who did obey the instruction was paired to a Lib Dem MP, Jo Swinson".

"There is some informal pairing which is at the discretion of the Whips. The Whips have total power. And the Whips will have made some arrangement that they were not prepared to make for me for when my daughter was in the theatre or for when my husband needed to be discharged. And for me, if there is one more thing I'd like to do, I even wrote to the Speaker and said 'Can't you have an arbitration system where at sudden short notice, genuinely, an MP needs to put a family member first? It's an emergency, and you will have some others. I mean, you can pair us up, instead of messing around with Whips misleading other Whips.' And the answer was 'no'. Even when I came in here 20 years ago, my predecessor drank himself to death, as far as we know, he was found dead, anyway. Alcohol".

"That was Ian Mills, and everyone knew he had a drink problem, sadly, but they didn't manage to sort it before he took his life, and I was so shocked by that. One of the first things I said to the Chief Whip on arrival was: 'surely you should have stepped in and saved this man's life? He must have needed to have gone into rehab? And surely you should have something like compassionate pairing?' And the answer was 'no'. So, that's my magic wand, I would change that. Because the stress on the family…. It's made me realize that, as I said to my husband, 'we're both 60 now, and there's me thinking it gets easier, and these things won't arise', when of course either of us could fall sick suddenly, as his major problem showed. I am in a job with no bandwidth at all for genuine family disasters, which happen".

Appointment by patronage rather than experience
Sarah: "There are a lot of things I would change. I would look at further diversifying Parliament. I am also concerned at the way patronage works in this place. The one thing that did

surprise me when I came here is that there is little professional development, like you would have in the NHS, when I used to teach junior doctors and medical students, professional development was part of the job. Whereas here, the only thing you are performance-managed on is whether you turn up and vote for the government".

"The trouble is, you can have people who are really passionate about a subject. They come into Parliament, but when appointments to committees are made, there's no opportunity to submit a CV or to be considered for a role on your merits, it's on who you know, the way that patronage works. So, if you look at what happens with Select Committees and why they've become more influential, it's because we've changed to have them elected, so they weren't then appointed by patronage. They probably shouldn't be called Select Committees at all, because they are not selected by the Whips: the Select Committee chairs are elected by the whole House of Parliament".

"And I think that for everything else that happens, ministerial appointments and all the other appointments including party roles, they are all through patronage, and it would modernize this workplace enormously if there were an application process".

"You could still argue a case for some roles being directly appointed by the PM, but I think there could be much greater use of the idea of people actually applying for roles. I have long objected, and in fact the reason that I think the Parliamentary Private Secretary (PPS) role would have been difficult for me is that you're part of the payroll vote, and that weakens Parliament. So if you have too many PPS roles, you limit the ability of people to challenge the executive, and that's part of Parliament's role".

"You have to get things right, and I would like to see, across all political parties, more thought given to how you develop people's roles in scrutinizing legislation, rather than it being the kind of haphazard approach that we have at the moment. You wouldn't accept patronage in any other organization: can you imagine if you went to see your surgeon and your surgeon had been appointed by patronage rather than ability? Yet we don't really consider that at all in Parliament, which is something that I've always found surprising".

In July 2017, Jess Phillips called for an independent review into elections of Chairs of House of Commons Select Committees, due to the relatively low number of female candidates. To date, there still hasn't been a review. Is there likely to be a review in the near future?

Jess: "No! There's a group of people that are on the Speaker's Reference Group, of which I am one, and we do reviews into [and] constantly keep an eye on the diversity balance. Not just about gender, disability, LGBT, although we're really good on that, we're the gayest Parliament in the world! We also review the Scottish Parliament. So, we do the number-crunching. But it isn't just about the chairs, it's the members of the Select Committees which are still very much dominated by men. Apart from the only one that isn't, which is the Women and Equalities Select Committee.

"And also the people who go and give evidence. We monitor that, so I think in the Defence Select Committee and the Treasury Select Committee, 98% of the people who give evidence are men. As if there are no women experts on the economy or our Armed Forces haven't got women in them. So, it's the breaking of culture within those organisations as well, where maybe they should send women. So we monitor that sort of thing, but by no means is Parliament actually reviewing it. Parliament does naff all".

"The Speaker is good, it's his reference group that does this. And there's a thing called the Good Parliament Report, where we're aiming to implement those recommendations. That's what the reference group is, it's basically the implementation group for the Good Parliament Report, but yes, it's very slow. Sarah Childs made 43 recommendations in 2016 and she'll get four to three of them".

Positive discrimination
Jo: "I don't oppose positive discrimination. I did, then I changed my view in 2016, when the Scottish Lib Dems and then the UK Lib Dems passed motions about enabling all-women shortlists (AWS), which I ultimately supported. So I have a view which says it's better if it's not necessary, but sometimes it is. For example, the Women on Boards initiative, when Vince and I were leading it and we had Mervyn Davies at the head of the review, was an example where you could get very significant progress, but it took a significant amount of political leadership, we went from 12% of Women on Boards in 2011 to 25% by 2015".

See the interim findings of the Hampton Alexander Report[4] (announced in 19th Nov 2018) about boardroom diversity. The target was one-third of boardrooms should be female by 2020, and doubt was cast on whether this was going to be achieved, or would legislation be necessary to speed things up?

Jo: "So getting to 30% or 33% by 2020 in that context ought not to be problematic. But what we have seen, of course, is that progress has not continued at the same pace. There has certainly been stalling and part of that is about the political leadership necessary to drive things. On top of it, I don't believe those less restrictive measures will work, but if they do work, they're probably better, because they're working by changing minds rather than changing behaviours, where people can still end up being quite oppositional".

"So, in terms of boards, the target obviously should be 50%. And there's no harm in setting targets along the way that are staging posts, and I think we need to celebrate progress because it's important for motivation. But we need to keep our eye on the main prize, which is getting to equality, and sometimes what we do see, and I write about this in my book,[5] is that we benchmark against where we were rather than where we're going, so we're too self-congratulatory and pat ourselves on the back instead of saying 'well hang on a second, we're nowhere near 50%, we've still got a long way to go'".

"But there is a balance to be struck, and if people have been working hard at something and made great strides ahead, and you're still not at 50:50, then there's a place for having a big party to say we hoped to get to 25% within a four-year period, we've done that, so let's use that to spur us on to get to the next target. So I don't have a problem itself with the target of 33% by 2020, if we think that that is a challenging stretch target by 2020, but I do sort of ask the question: 'What's the plan after that? How do we get to 50% and how long will that take?'"

"And in different industries, that will also vary. If you're working in engineering, then part of your long-term strategy on how you get to equality is about getting more girls doing physics at school, and that's going to take longer. Because the work that you do now with six-year-olds isn't going to even translate into more A-level physics attempts for girls for a decade, and then it's probably another five or six years after that before those young women will then be entering the workforce to join engineering firms, and time after that before they then achieve more senior levels".

"There's still an issue with talent loss within engineering, so it's not only that long-term thing, but you know that's part of it. So, it's going to take longer to achieve equality at the top executive team in an engineering firm, for example, than it would in a law firm. If you're a law firm and you've had 50% plus graduates in law being women for more than two decades, the problem is not that there's a lack of qualified women who are lawyers that could take these roles, the problem is cultural, about your organization, and attrition when women become mothers and not enough support by the company for them then. So it's a different issue to address that, and arguably shouldn't take quite so long because you've already got qualified people within that particular discipline".

"So, you need to look with nuance at that specific industry or area, set challenging but achievable targets, and keep your eye on getting to 50%".

Author: "It was interesting listening to some of the excuses given on the radio when discussing the Hampton Alexander Report, some of which were pathetic, such as "all the good women have been snapped up" and "women couldn't understand complex issues". It just worries me that in 20 years' time, we'll be having the same conversation, not because there aren't enough talented women, but because there's no culture shift amongst these companies at board level. After all, the law firms used to say they didn't have the talent: now they have to admit they have the female talent, but it leaves when it gets to a certain seniority, probably because they have babies and the company doesn't do enough to retain them".

Jo: "I do agree, and as I say, I'm not necessarily against introducing legislation, but I think that the reason progress has stalled has been taking the foot off the pedal, in terms of the political will behind this project. And that you end up seeing these attitudes, it's good that they're being ridiculed, but they still exist, people do still hold these views, even though they now know they shouldn't say them. When these comments are held up for ridicule on the public radio, then mindsets will change".

"But there was an anecdote, which I refer to in my book, where I was at an event, which was a pro-equality event, and they had some men talking, which is good, talking about the things they had done in their companies to support women, and these were the people who considered themselves to be enlightened. And there was one guy who was recounting an experience that he was proud of where he was interviewing a woman for a promotion and they had decided that they were going to give her the job, and then just at the meeting where he was going to tell her that she had won the promotion, she said: 'I just want to let you know that I'm actually pregnant'. And he said: 'well, obviously she couldn't have that job, because we needed to fill that job then, 'but I made sure that I then worked with her, and we got her another role and ultimately she got her promotion'".

"And I thought 'you've just admitted, in a room full of people, to pregnancy discrimination, which has been illegal for decades, and you think this has been a good story about women!' And he was just oblivious to the fact that what he'd done was illegal as well as wrong".

"So I think that some of the people who've been trotting out those excuses, they don't even see the gender inequality, because it's so ingrained, and they don't think that that is what they're doing. So, you're right that there's a huge cultural job to be done here, to challenge those attitudes, and that's why I encourage people to do that at all levels. I mean, government has got a role, but we all need to be doing this".

MPs are weighed down with greater caseloads, turning into social workers

Some would argue this is happening more to female MPs than male, because (and this is a generalization) women tend to be more caring and can often empathise better with victims, since there is more likelihood that they will have been in the same position themselves or that they will more often know someone who has. Are some constituencies much needier than others? Does poverty breed needier citizens? Is there a case for more funding for more staff to deal with higher workloads in poorer constituencies?

Is there evidence that proves there is a higher workload amongst poorer constituents? Or are wealthy citizens just as needy, but in different ways? Would we get two tiers of MPs? Might job-sharing help to solve this, as Caroline Lucas of the Green Party has suggested? One MP to scrutinize legislation whilst the other cares for the constituents? But let's guess which gender would take the majority of the high-profile

Westminster posts and then leave the "caring for the constituent" posts to the women.

There is an excellent website, TheyWorkForYou,[6] which shows exactly what your MP is doing for you in an easy-to-read format. It gives voting records, recent appearances, a register of specific interests, current and previous offices held, positions on bill and Special Committees, and social media details. This excellent website could be further enhanced with details of MP's caseloads, their average time taken to reply, sick days, and possibly time spent scrutinizing legislation. It's not fair that those MPs who spend the most time blowing their own trumpets and talking to the media are assumed to be the hardest working or the most effective.

One almost feels that Parliament should be functioning like any other good employer, with a management structure, or at least mentoring structure, with MPs having regular appraisals to better guide them in their effectiveness. A number of MPs said that it is very easy to be busy but ineffective and to lose sight of what they were voted in to achieve, or just to be swept along by the government's plans and the excitement of Westminster and to lose sight of their own personal reasons and plans to make the world a better place.

References:

1. University of Bristol (2016) [online]. Available at: https://www.bristol.ac.uk/media-library/sites/news/2016/july/20%20Jul%20Prof%20Sarah%20Childs%20The%20Good%20Parliament%20report.pdf [accessed 21st August 2018].

2. 50:50 Parliament website (2018) [online]. Available at: https://5050parliament.co.uk/ [accessed 14th Nov 2018].

3. *The Guardian* (2018) [online]. Available at: https://www.theguardian.com/politics/2018/jul/19/tory-whip-julian-smith-urged-to-explain-pairing-breach-that-caused-serious-damage [accessed 10th August 2018].

4. Hampton Alexander Report (2018) [online]. Available at: https://ftsewomenleaders.com/wp-content/uploads/2018/11/HA-Review-Report-2018.pdf [accessed 30th Nov 2018].

5. Swinson, J. (2018). *Equal Power and How You Can Make It Happen*. London. Atlantic Books.

6. They Work for You website (2018) Available at: https://www.theyworkforyou.com [accessed 26th May 2019].

Chapter 10

"No-one can quite imagine what a gender equal world would look like, that's why we're all too scared to go there."
-Jude Kelly, Women of the World Festival, London, 2015.

Long-term measures to get more women into Parliament?
As Jude Kelly said: "No-one on earth lives in a gender equal society. Why do women stay in this situation? Because we have nowhere else to go. There is no other gender equal world to go to, if there was, we'd all be flocking there. Can you imagine such a place? We should put time into thinking what a gender equal society would look like.

Making society gender-equal is scary for everyone. Men worry they would have to give too much of their power away. And many women think they would lose their power too, because too many women rely on the only power they have been able to get, which has been by 'sexing themselves up'. They can't imagine what other power they might be able to exert (especially those who have no education or career). We would all have to change the way we live and new norms would be created. Perhaps because this change is so great, no-one can imagine it. Simply because women make up 50% of society, the step looks too large."

Some of the more creative types have made YouTube videos which have shocked viewers. The hidden camera filming the woman walking the streets of New York,[1] the "This Girl Can" video,[2] the "Dove: Onslaught" advertising campaign,[3] the Australian "If a Man Lived Like a Woman for a Day" video:[4] all help to make the opposite sex realize what it is like to be a woman. Every day, we accept treatment that is "normal" when it isn't. Could we imagine ourselves in Saudi Arabia and accepting that we weren't allowed to drive? Could we accept living in Edwardian society when women weren't allowed to vote?

Everydaysexism has been hugely successful in highlighting everyday normalized sexism. This is a world where the power difference has been so distorted for so long that we all need to work to change it. It often takes younger generations to actually spot the normalized behaviour that older women can't recognize as being sexist. It took an Argentinian woman, Caroline Criado-Perez, to spot that there were no images of women, aside from the Queen, on any UK bank notes, and then to fight to do something about it. It was also Caroline who spotted that there were no female statues in Parliament Square. No British woman had even noticed the 18 male statues (including some obscure foreigners like Jan Smuts) as being anything other than the norm. Now we have one (Millicent Fawcett), most people will consider this as equality.

How long until we get a second woman statue in Parliament Square?

Long-term measures

Media misrepresentation of female politicians
There are many studies which focus on the media misrepresentation of women. Media sexism both reflects sexism in society (media reproducing sexism) and portrays a more gender-segregated picture than reality (media producing sexism), such that the media is a good measure of societal sexism, but also makes society more sexist than it would be otherwise.

There are also lots of definitions of sexism. UNESCO proposes "the supposition, belief or assertion that one sex is superior to the other, often expressed in the context of traditional stereotyping of social roles on the basis of sex, with resultant discrimination practiced against members of the supposedly inferior sex."

The Global Media Monitoring Project (GMMP) is the most reliable worldwide source for media coverage from a gender perspective. This shows that women currently make up 24% of news subjects globally (GMMP 2015); at the same time, women make up 23% of the world's national parliaments.[5]

Scholars emphasize that media sexism directly impacts female candidates' chances of success. Philo C. Wasburn and Mara H. Wasburn (2011) studied the case of Sarah Palin's vice-presidential campaign via the patterns of gendered reporting that have dissuaded women from entering politics. They identified five patterns: female candidates receive proportionally less coverage than male candidates; stories on female candidates focus more on aspects such as appearance and family; women are more likely to be trivialized and scrutinized in terms of their competence; women's policy positions on women's issues will be in focus, whether or not this is a policy area on which they stand; and their potential influence is questioned if they win.

Hillary Clinton faced a barrage of sustained media sexism during her 2016 presidential campaign,[6] to the extent that despite having years of relevant experience, a large financial war chest, family ties to power, name recognition, and party support at both stages of the election, she could not win against Trump, who had no experience and many more serious flaws.

Julia Gillard, the Australian prime minister from 2010 to 2013, had to face sustained sexism when on the campaign trail and in office. Her famous misogyny speech[7] against Tony Abbott went viral around the world.

The Effect of Media on Sexism study[8] also suggests that aside from the above, which focused on the intense three-week period prior to an election, that there is a longer-standing "bystander effect" built up over the years which causes women to discount the idea of going into politics because of ongoing sexist reporting.

Top five journalism gender traps[9]

Focusing on women's domestic life
Female candidates are often asked whether they can juggle their political responsibilities with their roles as mothers. For example, as *USA Today* wrote in 2014, "it's unclear how Chelsea's pregnancy will affect Hillary Clinton, who is considering a race for President in 2016". How many newspapers asked that question when Mitt Romney was proudly photographed with his 18 grandchildren or when George W. Bush and John McCain showed off theirs off to the press? That's right: zero.

Attaching them to powerful men
Another bias is to mention the "connections" that women must have needed to get themselves into politics. Women in power and those seeking public office are often portrayed as the inexpert delegates of influential men. For example, during the second administration of Spanish President Rodriguez Zapatero, 32- year- old Bibiana Aido was named Minister of Equality and Innovation, the youngest person to ever hold that position. To announce the news, the daily *El Pais* newspaper

ran the condescending headline "Dad, they're going to make me a minister!" and the copy below clarified that Aido came with guarantees from Rubalcaba and Felipe Gonzalez (two powerful male government officials).

Saying women get emotional

The media frequently questions the stability of female politicians, based on the stereotype that women are creatures of emotion. *Perfil*, an Argentinian political analysis magazine, dedicated a 2014 issue to the conflicts and judgement errors hounding then-President Cristina Fernandez. The title, "Cristina's emotional default", hinted that she was suffering from a mood disorder.

Discussing their looks

The media around the world is obsessed with the looks of female politicians and females in general. Why is this? Because the majority of journalists and editors are young men (nothing to do with their paying customers). The media judges women's physical appearance, granting obsessive attention to their clothing, makeup, and hairstyles. In 2008, Angela Merkel's cleavage caused an international stir at an Oslo opera house gala, with the *Daily Mail*, amongst others, publishing a photo of her with the headline "Merkel's weapons of mass distraction".

Commenting on their voices

During the 1950s and 1960s, women were kept from being commentators on the BBC, which said that their voices were too harsh and shrill for its broadcast medium. These views were finally discredited and women were reluctantly allowed to go on air as journalists and commentators, but in fewer numbers, paid much less than men, and given inferior or supporting roles. The BBC is notably still paying its female journalists far less, and after Carrie Gracie (head of the Chinese news desk) discovered she was paid 50% less than her counterparts on the Middle East and American news desks, she resigned. Her story of bullying and gagging orders by the BBC is disgraceful.

The treatment of female politicians has been similar, with many, including Margaret Thatcher and Hillary Clinton, having to face criticism of their voices; both had voice coaching.

Two studies by "Name It, Change It[10]" show that when papers comment on the physical appearance of women and/or use sexist rhetoric, they negatively impact how voters view women in numerous ways. Female candidates may be perceived as less likeable, empathetic, trustworthy, effective, or qualified. Candidates' favourability ratings drop and people become less inclined to vote for them. How can journalists do better?

(1) Apply the rule of reversibility. If you wouldn't ask it of a man, then don't ask it of a woman. If you wouldn't say it about a male candidate, then don't say it about his female counterpart.
(2) Don't focus on the private lives of women seeking public office.
(3) Train more journalists around the globe to recognize and eschew harmful gender stereotypes.

Long-term measures
Anne Milton: "The question is around how women define success, isn't it? One of the issues around the gender pay gap is that salary is a male-orientated measure of success. Women don't measure their success simply by their salary, they've got a more mixed bag of success measures. This might include their house and their children. As a woman, I would be

delighted that amidst all this hard governmental work, getting the armchair in the kitchen re-covered would be a major success for me. Money matters to women but so do other things."

"Long-term measures: you'd have to entirely change society, because women are always going to worry more about decorating the downstairs loo. We are more domestically orientated, whether we like it or not. Not many men will derive the pleasures that I will from re-covering an armchair, so it's not just about my job. If I could only do my job and not that other domestic stuff, I would find it frustrating. It took me a year and a half to find a person to do the downstairs loo. This just doesn't bother my husband that much...so we measure our success in different ways."

"I would love it if this place was 50:50. I think that individual MPs have a duty and a responsibility to recruit others, the difficulty is the adverse effects we now have of social media and a lot of other barriers such as childcare. Most women have quite a lot of self-respect, and they will say to themselves 'hmmm, why should I?' You can have lots of well-paid jobs, but as an MP, you get a chance to make a difference".

"And we put too much upon ourselves, we don't give up ground. We don't allow our husbands to do things that they are quite capable of doing. It's insulting to suggest that men can't do basic things around the house. Also, we don't delegate enough. To suggest your husband can't manage the washing machine.... I just feel uncomfortable with that, but that's my problem, not his".

Heidi: "Theresa May started Women2Win a number of years ago, and that works well, they offer coaching, training, and speech-making practice. It's a network for putting people in touch who can help you. That's morphed into #AskHerToStand, which is the latest iteration. You can have that machinery in the background, but it's up to every one of us. When I meet somebody who I think can be an MP, I ask them".

"I do it on the doorstep in my constituency, if I'm having a good argument with somebody, I'll say, 'you're right, you'd be great at this job, why don't you apply? But clearly not here!' But that's what you do, you lead by example. The more normal people we have in here, and different people, the more representative it will be of the UK, and then maybe people won't hate politicians so much, because we'll sound a bit more like they do".

Change the 1950s social policy around the family
Jess: "The long-term measure for women in literally everything – economics, independence, political representation, ending violence – is always the liberation of women. We have to, we are not liberated yet. We have to change the fact that we still have a lesser position in society. And that's like the panacea to everything. One of the really good long-term measures that we could instigate is a change in the 1950s social policy around the family. And we should equalize men's rights and roles over children in the family. They should have paternity leave at the same level as exists for maternity".

"I don't know why we have 1950s legislation that basically says, yes, women should take loads of time off work looking after their children, just because we give birth to them...other people can look after them."

Jo Swinson

"In the medium- to long-term, there are also structural changes needed in terms of Parliament. There's been improvements in terms of family life, putting a nursery on-site, a crèche is shortly going to open, bringing in proxy voting for MPs who are parents, if they've got young children or a recently adopted child. Those things are helpful in terms of continuing that progress".

"But also, the electoral system is something which we know having the single-member constituency system, that while the constituency link is important and I would want to keep that, having multi-member constituencies like you do in local government or in the Scottish Parliament, Welsh Assembly, and so on, those ways can certainly tend to encourage more women, because it's more obvious if you're just standing a slate of all-male candidates, whereas if you're just putting up one candidate per constituency, that's one of the things that's often less noticeable".

"Issues that I'm particularly interested in, now, specifically post-financial crash and having reflected on time in government as well, I think we're living in an economy that needs quite radical reform since it's not working for too many people. I'm keen on doing policy work to find out what some of those radical reforms need to be. I don't believe it's Jeremy Corbyn's prescription of going back to the 1970s, but I don't think it's business as usual either. Things that we started doing when I was in the Department for Business on employee ownership and improved boardroom culture."

"But I'm quite keen to further develop that thinking, to see how we can change the way our economy works and the way in which business operates. And separate to that, following on from a major speech that Vince Cable did on technology and artificial intelligence in the wider economy, because again, this is an area where we need to be thinking through regulation, ethics, and what are the policy responses to these massive changes in how the workforce will be, in how our daily lives will be, governed by technology."

"There are huge opportunities, but also big risks, and on both of these main issues, the kind of wider economic reform and technology and its progress, because Brexit is such a dominating political theme, these issues are getting very little wider political attention in terms of policy change, so yes, I'm trying to do some quite interesting thinking, and hopefully coming up with some quite radical policy positions on these issues to take forward. So that's where my long-term thinking and views are at the moment."

"And regarding company law, if you look at directors' duties, then there's already a clause which says that a CEO should have some responsibility towards the community, not just the share price, even though nearly all CEOs just care about the latter. So the more fascinating question is why is it still interpreted in the way that it is? And what is the best way to change that behaviour? To change that clause a bit? I can't remember what section it is of the Companies Act, but there already is a very well-worded element of that, and you think, oh well, that does the job. But changing the culture, that it's all about next week's share price, is a much harder thing to achieve than that piece of wording."

"So, I'm on the advisory board of an organization called Blueprint for Better Business, and there's some good thinking going on with some of these issues, but changing these cultural certainties is quite a challenge. And of course, better diversity is part of that, because it starts to bring in different

229

perspectives and challenges things that have been deemed to be the status quo in the way that it was done. And when you start challenging that in one area, it's easier to challenge that across the board."

Rosie: "I suppose it's a societal shift. Seeing more women in the House is going to make more women realize it's a job for them. We know that local councils need more women. Interesting women in those ideas and making them realize that they can make a difference in their own community, that's really important".

"I know there's been a hostile atmosphere in some local councils. That's not necessarily an atmosphere you want to be in. I know many women Councillors who sit when they have their budget meetings until 11pm, 12pm, 1am, and then have to get up for a job the next day, that's utterly ridiculous. Nobody needs to be there or making decisions and voting on things at 11, 12 o' clock at night. What decisions should you be making then? How is that conducive to normal life? So, all of those things need to be looked at. Political meetings go on during the week, late at night. Ridiculous again, let's change all of that."

Caroline: "It's a combination of modernizing Parliament so that it actually sits in a sensible way that is doable with family life and what it involves. Other parliaments seem quite capable of doing that. The Swedish Parliament has 50:50 men and women who work 9am to 5pm. Why not? What's the problem? But there's a sort of machismo around the fact 'can I stay up later than you?' Presenteeism is a problem in British culture generally, which is quite a misogynist culture. It's not me saying that, Jeremy Paxman used my case as an illustration in his book *The English*[11], where I was rejected by 27 constituencies, and he uses it as an example that it's still very difficult for women to come into politics".

"Yes, there is definitely a misogynistic press, you ask the lobby here in Parliament. There are very few female journalists in Parliament. There are not that many female political journalists, with a few exceptions, Laura Kuenssberg has done quite well, but look at the trolling she's had".

"It's just so difficult, and what is that about? We need to look deeper into our nation's heart and soul to understand that. Occasionally, when I've been on the end of it, I've just said to my husband, 'what is the problem?'".

"I have had some trolling myself, but being the Second Church Estates Commissioner, it's a bit like being a Minister of State without the hassle. You're not so much in the front line. When you are really in the front line is when you come in for trolling".

Female role models and more statues of women?
The Public Monuments and Sculpture Association (PMSA)[12] has been recording public sculptures across the UK for three decades, although its database is not an exhaustive record of all statues in the country. Of the 828 statues it listed in April 2018, 174 were female, or one in five. But this doesn't tell the whole story. Only 80 (or 46%) of these were named women, whereas out of the 534 male statues, 422 were named (79%).

Taking headless women (nymphs) and naked women out of the equation, even amongst the 80 female figures with names, 15 are mythical or fictional and 38 of them are royal, Queen Victoria being the most common.

So, named female statues, of real, not royal women, comprise a mere 27, or 3%. The situation with the named Blue Plaque scheme is not a lot better, with women comprising just 127 out of 931 plaques (13%). When your author first typed "named women statues" into google around 2015, it came back with: "do you mean naked women statues?" There has been some progress since then, in 2019 it no longer does this and actually comes up with a relevant list.

Chi: "Growing up in the 1970s and 1980s, there weren't any female role models in politics, it was very male and very middle and upper class. I think my role model would be my mother and then in terms of groups, I was hugely influenced by African Americans like Maya Angelou and Bell Hooks."

"When I'm bringing young people from Newcastle and showing them round Parliament, then I feel that I'm followed around by dead white men, because that is the overwhelming representation of portraits and group scenes that you see in Parliament, particularly in the Palace of Westminster. Portcullis House is slightly better, and I have raised this issue with the House of Commons Commission and the House of Commons Art Commission, who are responsible for artwork. I'm told they're looking to change or evolve it, but change is extremely slow, and I don't think that my constituents should travel all the way from Newcastle just to see people whom they can never identify with".

Jo: "In politics, female role models that have inspired me include Shirley Williams, and outside of politics, or politics with a small "p" perhaps, Anita Roddick. I was very taken by her vision of how business can operate as a force for good in society. That is an important idea, which is too often lost in the short-term pursuit of share price and profit, regardless of how it is achieved. Businesses need to make a profit, but the stakeholders that a business has goes much wider than their shareholders, and Anita Roddick saw that and put it into practice and I find that very inspirational. She was a very inspiring woman".

Parliament UK produced its first ever Gender Sensitive Parliament Audit[13] on 26th November 2018, which, like Professor Sarah Childs' Good Parliament Report, makes for fascinating reading and offers 52 recommendations to make both houses more gender equal. Select committees in both the upper and lower houses have no requirement for gender balance, and 32 out of 36 Commons select committees and 29 out of 32 Lords select committees are majority male. The paper acknowledges that whilst women make up only 32% and 26% of both the lower and upper houses respectively, they could not realistically make up equal percentages of the select committees, since this would put too much strain on the existing female MPs.

Many other recommendations are made in terms of sitting hours, support with childcare, better processes to deal with sexual harassment and culture, maternity and paternity leave, proxy voting, crèche facilities, more paintings and busts of women, more female toilets, and a culture that mainstreams gender equality. A brief read of this report indicates we still have a long way to go.

References:

1.YouTube (2015) [online]. Available at: https://www.youtube.com/watch?v=b1XGPvbWn0A [accessed 5th Aug 2018].

2. YouTube (2014) [online]. Available at:
https://www.youtube.com/watch?v=jsP0W7-tEOc
[accessed 2nd July 2016].

3. YouTube (2008) [online]. Available at:
https://www.youtube.com/watch?v=9zKfF40jeCA
[accessed 1st June 2010].

4. YouTube (2019) [online]. Available at:
https://www.youtube.com/watch?v=JIjnD2bG0gU
 [accessed 10th Mar 2019].

5.Inter Parliamentary Union website (2019) [online].
Available at: www.ipu.org [accessed 3rd April 2019].

6. Sage Journals (2018) [online]. Available at:
https://journals.sagepub.com/doi/full/10.1177/237802311773
2441 [accessed 2nd Dec 2018].

7.YouTube (2013) [online]. Available at:
https://www.youtube.com/watch?v=EvWTamyxKlA
[accessed 5th June 2014].

8. Haraldsson, A. and Wangnerud, L. (May 2018). *Journal of Feminist Media Studies*. "The Effect of Media Sexism on Women's Political Ambition: Evidence from a Worldwide Study." Available at: www.tandfonline.com
[accessed 28th Jan 2019].

9. *The Conversation* (2017). "Five Ways the Media Hurts Woman – And How Journalists Everywhere Can Do Better" [online]. Available at: http://theconversation.com/five-ways-the-media-hurts-female-politicians-and-how-journalists-everywhere-can-do-better-70771 [accessed 25th Jan 2019].

10. NameITChange website. (2019). [online]. Available at:
http://www.nameitchangeit.org/ [accessed 1st Oct 2019]

11. Paxman, J. (2007). *The English: A Portrait of a People*.
London. Penguin Books.

12. BBC News (2018) [online]. Available at:
https://www.bbc.co.uk/news/uk-43884726
[accessed 24th April 2019].

13. Parliament UK (2018) [online]. Available at:
https://www.parliament.uk/business/news/2018/december/g
ender-sensitive-parliament-audit-published-today--/
[accessed 10th May 2019].

Acknowledgements

Huge thanks is given to all those people who generously gave up their time to speak to me and passed on their thoughts and wisdom, specifically to the 12 sitting Members of Parliament who, despite their very busy working lives and the fact that I wasn't their constituent, still gave me lengthy interviews and extensive insight into the workings of Parliament and what it is actually like to be a female MP in Parliament today. So much thanks to the following MPs: Anne Milton, Dame Caroline Spelman, Justine Greening, Heidi Allen, Sarah Wollaston, Jess Phillips, Rosie Duffield, Chinyelu Onwurah, Anneliese Dodds, Kate Green, Lisa Cameron, Jo Swinson, Preet Gill, Margot James, and Gillian Martin, SNP.

Also much thanks to John Bercow, who so generously encouraged me to write this book at the start and offered me a long list of contacts. He has been a huge stalwart in improving better gender representation in Parliament.

Also, much thanks to other contributors, including:
Professor Sarah Childs, Birkbeck, University of London, author of "The Good Government"
Professor Palie Smart, Head of School, University of Bristol
Professor Drude Dahlerup, University of Stockholm
Sara Passmore, University of Oxford
Nan Sloane, Centre for Women and Democracy
Alex Meakin, PhD Research Associate, University of Sheffield
Lee Chalmers, Co-founder of the Parliament Project
Frances Scott, Founder of 50:50 Parliament
Candy Piercy, Campaign for Gender Balance, Liberal Democrat Party
Jenny Robinson, Henley Business School
Jade Thomas, Eau Rouge Design for the wonderful book cover

Kats Handel for exceptional proof reading
Stephanie Solywoda, Director, Stanford University in Oxford
Jacqui Smith, former Home Secretary
Iain Dale, Biteback Publishing
Stephanie Baxter
Jenny Robinson
Julie Brash
Anna Skinner
Lyndon Stotesbury
Andrew Green
Kat Lee

Also to many other friends and family for ongoing practical and
moral support who are too numerous to mention.
You know who you are.

About the author

Hilary Baxter has had a career of thirty plus years working in marketing and business development roles in both UK and international companies. With an undergraduate degree from St Andrews University and a Masters from Imperial College, she has also set up and run two companies of her own.

She has been an armchair feminist all of her life, but seeing her own daughter and son's generation being as gender stereotyped as her own, made Hilary devote more time to the cause of equality.

Hilary is a Founding Member of the Women's Equality Party and the Fawcett Society and has spoken regularly in Oxford Colleges about gender equality and especially the pay gap.

Printed in Poland
by Amazon Fulfillment
Poland Sp. z o.o., Wrocław